Flight Club

Rebel, Reinvent, and Thrive: How to Launch Your Dream Business

Felena Hanson

Founder of Hera Hub

"This is your boarding pass to fly entrepreneur class. A must read for every woman who is thinking about launching a business!"

~Ali Brown - entrepreneur, coach, angel investor, featured on ABC's Secret Millionaire *show*

Limits of Liability and Disclaimer of Warranty

The authors and publisher shall not be liable for your misuse of this material. This book is strictly for informational and educational purposes.

Warning-Disclaimer

The purpose of this book is to educate and entertain.

ISBN-13: 978-0692674697
ISBN-10: 0692674691

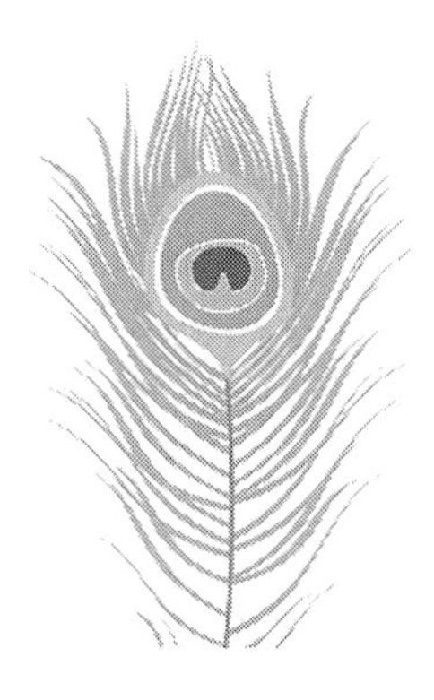

I want to connect with you!

Tell me what you think of the book by…

- Emailing me at Felena@FlightClubBook.com
- Posting your thoughts and questions on www.Facebook.com/FlightClubBook
- Connecting with me at www.Twitter.com/FelenaHanson

Ready to launch your business?
Get a FREE subcription to our online platform -
go to www.StepsToStartup.com today!

Even if you've already taken flight, there are likely new things to learn among the dozens of tips, tools and resources in this unique tutorial.

Looking forward to getting to know you!

Felena

Contents

You can't connect the dots looking forward; you can only connect them looking backwards. So you have to trust that the dots will somehow connect in your future. You have to trust in something - your gut, destiny, life, karma, whatever. This approach has never let me down, and it has made all the difference in my life.

- Steve Jobs

An Invitation To A Journey

I'm inviting you to share in my journey—one filled with rebellion, reinvention, independence, diplomacy, and (perhaps most important of all) collaboration. You'll gain a firsthand experience of the challenges, successes, and wisdom I've gained over the last 40 years. We're also going to get down to the nitty-gritty—the nuts and bolts of business—and how I was able to build something tangible yet sincere (a word not often associated with business) by creating Hera Hub.

My life story may come across as a bit scattered and tumultuous at times; however, as you'll soon see, everything I've done—from selling peacock feathers as a child, to surviving a near-fatal car accident, to sustaining three professional setbacks—has led to my life's work of providing women with a strong platform and a supportive community from which to launch and grow their businesses.

Whether you believe the prediction that more than 50 percent of the knowledge-based workforce will be independent by 2020 or not, it's clear that the world is changing, and with this change comes the need to think like an entrepreneur. My hope is that by sharing my journey, and the experience of other accomplished women, I will inspire you to take charge of your career and, ultimately, your destiny. It's your turn to take flight!

My best!

Felena

Part One: Felena's Story

Chapter 1
Rebellion

AS FAR BACK AS I can remember my life has progressed along a very unconventional path. It began when I was just 18 months old and my parents purchased a unique piece of property on the Central Coast of California, located near the edge of a small town called Arroyo Grande.

That old house was ripe for fueling a child's creativity and imagination. It was dilapidated in a peaceful kind of way and sat on two acres of land that consisted of pine trees, an orchard, a duck pond, and an old bus-repair barn. All of that, coupled with the creek that ran alongside the property, made it feel like my very own *Little House on the Prairie*.

I loved living in that country house (as I still like to think of it), running around the property, surrounded by nature. Along with the usual suspects of dogs and cats, we also had horses, ducks, and even a mating pair of peacocks that my mother named Mr. and Mrs. Peabody. In our house every animal was given a proper name—at one point we had 60 goats and dozens of chickens that all had their own names! I think it was my mom's way of showing respect and acknowledging that animals were very much part of the family.

As it turned out, Mr. Peabody was quite mean. He would walk around the yard with a bit of a scowl (if that's possible for a bird), chasing and pecking at my friends and me. I don't know how my mom didn't see this as dangerous, as he had some seriously combative-looking spurs on the back of his legs!

Aside from his cantankerous disposition, Mr. Peabody had a beautiful display of feathers that he'd often show off to attract Mrs. Peabody's attention. It was like a lion's mane, giving him his strength. Every fall, when he naturally shed his feathers, it almost seemed like he would lose his mojo and mope around the yard, looking dejected.

But Mr. Peabody's loss was my gain, for each fall I would run about gathering up his dropped feathers so I could turn around and sell them at the corner store for $1 each. Considering this was the late seventies—with the flamboyant disco era in full swing and the Bee Gees on constant rotation—it's not surprising that they sold like hotcakes.

Mr. Peabody

Although there was a part of me that envied my friends who received a weekly allowance, my parents (along with the help of Mr. Peabody) succeeded in teaching me at a very young age that money is not gifted, but rather earned. With landslide earnings of almost $80 to stash away in my pocket that first day out, I felt a wave of excitement and independence wash over me—my entrepreneurial roots were planted!

Roots Run Deep

Looking back to the major influencers of my early entrepreneurial spirit, it's clear to see that the roots run deep. Besides my parents, my grandpa Hanson was one of those influences. He was by far one of the most creative people in my life—a "nutty professor" of sorts. You could always find him in his converted garage behind his house, surrounded by every kind of random object and contraption (a.k.a. junk). As a kid, it was the coolest thing in the world to join him in his routine treasure hunts at the local thrift store or garage sale.

Although grandpa Hanson spent the bulk of his career in the accounting industry, a rebel streak often surfaced in some very unconventional and varied ways. For instance, he was always engineering that garage full of junk to create something interesting, like a self-driving three-wheel bicycle (complete with an American flag and an accompanying stream of marching music) or his own makeshift solar panels that he precariously mounted on the roof, which never really worked.

His love of unique mechanical contraptions extended to later in life when, as a World War II veteran, he purchased and refurbished a vintage fire truck so he could show it off in all of the local veteran's parades. As you'll discover later, his owning this fire truck would prove to be rather ironic in the context of my life story.

Grandfather's fire truck

About 25 years into his career my grandfather flexed his entrepreneurial muscles, leaving accounting to buy a small building where he started a mailing business in Fresno, California; which in turn influenced my dad's own career path.

As young newlyweds, both my mom and dad dropped out of college to start a new life together on the Central Coast of California. They both wanted to do anything to get out of the Fresno heat. Driven to provide for his new family, my dad tried anything he could to earn money and make ends meet. Like his father, he started a business in the ever-so-glamorous field of addressing junk mail. One weekend on a trip back to the Central Valley my Grandfather convinced my dad to take several rolls of carpet back with him to try to sell in his refurbished bus barn. This effort eventually led to success and, after many years of hard work, my dad has a thriving retail floor-covering business.

Because his business was literally next door to our house, my dad was constantly working. He was always on the move, building something new, making improvements here or there and fixing things around our property. The thing I remember most is that he was always eager to teach me new things and encouraged me to get involved in whatever he was doing. I don't think I remember him ever sitting on the couch and just relaxing!

Interestingly, my mom was similar—she was a hard worker and was always building and fixing things—yet at the same time, she was completely opposite from my dad. She is the most elegant, talented, problem-solver I know.

While my mom didn't "work" outside the home during the first seven years of my life, she certainly wasn't spending any time on the couch either. In fact, she was responsible (for the most part) for building—not contracting out, but actually building—the second story of our modest home and a barn at the back of our two-acre lot. Besides her over-the-top projects, my mom supported my dad in the business, raised me, and was also very involved in our community church choir and other performing arts, like community theater.

All of these activities gave me a profound respect for her and helped me to grow up as a fiercely independent and resourceful child. No Barbie Dolls for me; my life was filled with Tonka trucks, unconventional pets, and anything else resourceful and "non-girly."

In the end, my parents' marriage wasn't successful—another life event to which I attribute my fierce independence. I'm not quite sure why my parents married, as they were so completely different from each other. After eight years of giving it a go—most of which was spent bitterly and openly fighting—they filed for divorce. I always remember thinking that I never wanted to be in that position, but that *was* indeed the position I would be in 23 years later.

Despite the battle, I still feel lucky. At one point, when my mother moved us three hours away, my dad would drive six hours round-trip just so he could spend time with me for his "every other weekend" rights. He would sometimes even drive down just to see me on random Saturdays if he wasn't able to spend the entire weekend with me. This was without fail for two years!

One thing was certain: I had two parents who loved me dearly and continued to fight over custody until the day I was legally able to make my own decision. Not all parents, especially dads, would fight so hard to spend time with their daughters. By showing me that they loved me unconditionally, my parents instilled in me a strong sense of self and, by making me work for everything I received, helped me become confident in my abilities rather than developing a sense of entitlement. This combination has given me a true sense of self-worth, which has gotten me through some extremely difficult times.

New Beginnings

My mom was, and still is, brave! When my parents divorced, my mom (at age 30) dove headfirst into a new career and built a new life for herself. Heading back to school, she joined a specialized two-year program for Exotic Animal Training and Management in Moorpark, California.

After graduating and accepting a position as the manager of the Atascadero Zoo, my mom moved us back to the Central Coast. Shortly after moving back she began attending a local church and met Steve McConnell, who was a warden at the local youth prison. Soon thereafter they began dating and quickly married. Little did I know, within that very same year, my dad would also meet and marry the next love of his life, Susan Davis, who he had met at his own church.

Although I grew up as an only child for the first nine years of my life, that all was about to change! With my parents' new marriages came births and adoptions, and I gained eight new brothers and sisters over the course of three years. This time marked the start of an entirely new and impactful phase of my life—one filled with new stepparents, new siblings, and … *tigers.*

Yes, We Had Tigers!

While I was a latchkey kid in third and fourth grade, I was a zoo kid in fifth and sixth grade. Every day after school I took the bus to the zoo to help my mom with her afternoon duties, including caring for all the animals. It was amazing!

The pinnacle of my adventures at the zoo was when the resident male and female tigers bred and gave birth to two adorable baby tiger cubs. To my mother's dismay, the female tiger rejected her cubs soon after giving birth (perhaps she was perturbed that she was being held in captivity—can't say I blame her!) As the manager of the zoo, my mom had no choice other than to bring the two cubs home to bottle-feed them for several months.

You can't imagine how fast these tigers grew! From the palm of your hand to bigger than our dogs in a matter of weeks!

I feel beyond lucky to have had this experience, and I cherish the memories of having two tiger cubs run around our five acre property. Can you imagine the conversations I had at school? "Would you like to come over this afternoon and see my two baby tigers?"

Getting down and dirty working at the zoo and taking care of the animals helped me shed any sense of false pride at a very early age. Diving in and doing whatever was needed deeply influenced how I moved through the world. Even now, if someone comes into Hera Hub and asks me what I do, I often respond with sassy good humor, "I'm the janitor. I scrub the toilets." Truth be told, I don't mind getting my hands dirty with the best of them!

Exploring The World

As a young adult working in my father's business, I found I had a knack for sales and creativity. The logic of business just clicked with me from an early age. Although I was involved in my high school's business club (DECA), I wasn't a very dedicated student. In fact, I earned mostly *C*s throughout my young academic life. Apparently, I was far too interested in boys than class! One of those boys was Ryan Ripley, a handsome young man who was 4-years older than me. He worked for the local fire department and lived just down the street. We dated my junior and senior year, but we broke up right after high school because I felt I needed to experience other relationships. I just seemed to have something for fire trucks, as you will see again at another critical juncture in my life.

Not having bachelor's degrees themselves, my parents never pushed me to go to college. In fact, my dad hated school; he found it impractical and a waste of time. Because of this, he gave me a choice: he would either pay for college or I could take the same chunk of money and use it to start my own business or put a down payment on a home. Since I realized I wasn't savvy enough to invest in a home or start my own business, I decided it was wiser to continue my education.

Since my GPA wasn't adequate to get into a decent college, I decided to attend the local community college for two years with the goal of transferring to a four-year school. I thrived in this new environment, and I was able to improve my grades and focus on the subjects I enjoyed. Much to my delight, my grades earned me entrance into a well-respected private school, the University of San Diego (USD).

One of my weakest subjects at USD was foreign languages. I was able to get around my foreign-language requirement in high school, but the college requirement was looming over me. I couldn't pass Spanish to save my life!

Miraculously, I was able to convince my dad to allow me to do my language requirement in Spain through a study-abroad program (I promised to pay him back, which I did.) This three-month experience was to be one of my defining moments as a young adult, teaching me just as much (if not more) about myself than the Spanish language.

I immersed myself in the Spanish culture for two months, and then I traveled around Western Europe for an additional month. Not knowing a single soul when I arrived in Spain, I was lucky enough to meet a number of great girls from all over the United States, including Shawna.

Shawna and I traveled through Spain, Italy, Switzerland, and France together for three adventurous, laughter-filled weeks. When the time came for her to return home, I was faced with being abroad one more week … solo. At 20 years old—having never ventured outside the United States on my own before—this was where the *rubber really met the road*!

Without sharing the situation with my parents, I decided to go it alone. The day that Shawna left Paris to return back to the U.S.,

I put my Eurail pass to good use and hopped on a night train to Munich, Germany. I remember the whirring sound of the tracks and the rocking of the train as I slipped in and out of sleep, my young mind ever wary of the luggage thieves I had been warned about.

I arrived in Munich the next morning without incident and set off to explore the city. I had no idea that this day would turn into my defining "adult" moment. After walking around for a few hours, I found an open area with multiple picnic tables. A beautiful woman approached me and asked if I would like to order a beer. The question startled me a bit as it was about 11am. Apparently I had landed square in the middle of a beer garden. I did what any 20 year-old American would do and said "Ja! Na sicher!"

As I sat there sipping my pint, I remember feeling so free! (This was well before I had a cell phone or even email) "*No one* knows where I am. I'm an adult—I have arrived!" I drifted around the city for the day, slightly tipsy, exhilarated by my new found freedom.

As it turns out, I'm the only one in my family—out of eight brothers and sisters and both my parents—to earn a bachelor's degree. My undergraduate experiences helped me discover that I really loved school, and I ended up graduating from the University of San Diego with honors. And while my parents did not emphasize going to college, I knew they were proud.

Chapter 2
Reinvention

AS I MADE MY way through the checkout line in the grocery store, I heard an all-not-too-uncommon exclamation from behind me: "Wow, those are some pretty *crazy* scars you have there! I hope you don't mind me asking, but … what happened?"

When I turned around, I saw an incredulous look on the face of the man behind me, just waiting for my response. "Well, it is pretty *crazy*, but I used to skydive and about 15 years ago, during a jump, my parachute didn't open. Luckily, I lived to tell the tale, but now I have these scars to remind me—never jump out of a perfectly good airplane again!"

A few seconds passed by and I could see that he was trying to register what I had just said. All the man could get out was, "Wow. Really? ... That's really scary."

After a few more seconds of letting him squirm, I decided to let him off the hook. So, I followed up with a smile and said, "No, not really. Just joking! I was in a car accident and got hit by a fire truck. (Yes, a *fire truck*.)" As if this was any less incredible … however, it was the truth all the same.

Although I was *just* in a car accident, the deep scars and the reminders they carry are very real and powerful. Besides having titanium plates in my face, rods in my left arm and leg, and pins in my hips, scars are visible on my pretty much every extremity of my body. Every one of these scars is important to me, as they are reminders of how far I've come in life. What doesn't kill you makes you stronger!

How I Proudly Earned These Scars…

When I graduated from college in 1995 the economy was not at its peak. I had a challenging time finding a decent job within San Diego. Because of this, I ended up taking work and living in Los Angeles. At the time, I was madly in love with a young man I had met in college, Brian Taylor. Luckily, Brian was able to transfer to the University of California, Los Angeles (UCLA) to finish out his arts degree while I worked. I was happy!

Brian and I headed back down to San Diego one weekend. I dropped him off to see his family and I headed to the beach to spend the rest of the weekend with girlfriends I'd lived with while I was back at community college. I was so excited to see them, as we hadn't all been together in over three years!

I remember cruising along in my Volkswagen Jetta as Bob Marley pumped out the speakers, and the excitement of going to see my girls coursed through my body. I was grooving and my Saturday night was on!

As I approached the end of Interstate 8, right as it meets Sunset Cliffs, I looked ahead at the traffic light to see if I had the "green". I thought, "Wow, I never get a green light at the end of the 8!" This light is notorious for taking what feels like an eternity to turn from red to green.

And that's the last thing I remember…

What happened next changed my life forever. I never saw or heard the fire truck coming. The next thing I remember is waking up 24 hours later in the hospital.

As I later learned, the fire truck had run the red light and smashed into the front driver's side corner of my car as I sailed through the intersection. Not really a fair fight!

It took first responders close to an hour to use a crane to separate the fire truck from the carnage that was my car. Only then could they use the Jaws of Life, opening the top of my car like an oversized tuna can. In all, it took two hours to extract me from my car. I was immediately rushed by helicopter to the nearest hospital.

Although, thankfully, I was in shock and don't have a single recollection of what happened during or after the accident. My girlfriend's, who had found their way to the hospital by calling the Highway Patrol after I was hours late to meet them, later told me that I was very alert in the emergency room when they arrived.

Apparently I complained about the board behind my back and wanted to make sure someone took out my contacts. I was in such extreme shock that I clearly had no idea what was going on. The fact was, much of the left side of my body was crushed... getting my contacts out should have been the least of my worries!

Twelve hours of surgery later, I finally woke up to a group of what looked like a dozen or more doctors, nurses, and medical students standing around me. Apparently, I had been admitted into a teaching hospital and I was the case study of the week.

When my dad arrived at the hospital the next morning the doctors gave him the run-down of the damage and surgeries they had completed so far. They also shared their concern with the way my legs and pelvis had broken and thus the likelihood I may not be able to run again. This came as a particular shock to my dad, as I had developed a fairly strong passion for running during college—one that he now shared with me. We both had completed several marathons. I guess the information was just too much for him. He literally blacked out for a few moments.

I spent approximately two weeks at UCSD Hospital starting the long process of repair and recovery, and let me tell you, there was a lot of me to fix. I broke well over 20 bones in my arms, legs and face. They had to put titanium plates throughout my cheekbones, forehead, and palate. Many of my teeth were broken or knocked out completely, and the bridge of my nose was flattened. Ultimately, this area was rebuilt three times with bone taken from my hip. Before they could even get to these reconstructive surgeries, I had to undergo immediate surgery to relieve the pressure that the head injuries had placed on my brain. I also had a trachea tube for a week, making it impossible for me to speak. As a result, I resorted to writing notes in a notebook in order to communicate. Thinking back, I must have looked like Frankenstein's Bride!

I think the most powerful part of this experience was the new perspective that I, as well as everyone around me, gained. It's going to sound crazy, but to have the opportunity to simply appreciate life was worth all the pain and suffering (made a bit easier thanks to Morphine).

The support and outpouring of love I received from my family and friends during this time touched me to my core.

I think each one of us, in our own way, came to terms with the importance of living every day to the fullest, taking risks and following our hearts. Anything less than living our true life's purpose—to its fullest potential—was simply not good enough anymore.

Your time is limited; so don't waste it living someone else's life. Don't be trapped by dogma—which is living with the results of other people's thinking. Don't let the noise of others' opinions drown out your own inner voice. And most important, have the courage to follow your heart and intuition.

- Steve Jobs

Learning To Fly Again

After a month in the hospital, I began the painful, arduous, journey of rehabilitation. I spent several months in a wheelchair, working as hard as I could on a daily basis to rebuild my strength and muscle memory so I could walk again.

After I was transferred to Daniel Friedman Rehabilitation Hospital in Los Angeles, I received a phone call one day in my room. On the other end, I heard a young man explaining who he was and asking me how I was doing. It was a call from one of the paramedics who had helped me at the scene of my car accident. My situation had impacted him so deeply that I had remained on his mind, and he somehow managed to track me down. He simply said, "I just wanted to make sure you're okay." It took me a moment to process who this person was and why he was checking on me. After our brief conversation, I never saw or heard from him again, and yet it was through this conversation that I found out that I was conscious through the entire rescue. He said that I knew my name, my Social Security number, and where I was going that night. I was shocked (pun intended) by this news. Amazing how our body and mind can suppress!

Some months after my accident, I was handed all the documents that accompanied my case. In the box was a VHS tape labeled with the date of my accident - 5/4/1996. It was apparently standard for first responders to take video footage of a rescue—I'm assuming for training or liability purposes. I was home alone one night when curiosity got the best of me. I decided to pop in the tape. I immediately saw myself lying trapped in what was barely identifiable as my car. As I watched the surreal images flash before me, I could hear myself saying in a pained voice, "Somebody help me... Please, somebody help me." The second I saw and heard all of this, the experience and memory of the accident came powerfully flooding back. I couldn't believe it. It was like a file folder that had been shoved down into the recesses of my memory had been brought back up front and forward.

I immediately turned the video off, knowing in my heart that I didn't need (or want) to see this. I now realize how lucky I was that I was in shock after the accident, since the trauma I experienced could have had long-term psychological effects ... but it didn't. Thankfully, I'm not afraid to drive, I'm not afraid of fire trucks (although I do get out of their way when I see them coming!), and I haven't suffered from any form of posttraumatic stress.

Now I look fondly on my scars. They are here to remind me—every single day—how lucky I am to be here, alive and able to do something amazing with my life. I also believe that this "attitude of gratitude" was what helped me heal and get back on track so quickly.

Run, Felena, Run!

I'm proud to say, despite my doctors' initial nay saying, I am once again a runner! It took quite some time, as I literally had to learn how to walk again. I vividly remember one of my first attempts to walk. My family took me to the beach and rented a beach wheelchair from the Department of Parks and Recreation. I remember how fantastic it felt to get out of my regular wheelchair and into this dune buggy contraption, with my family by my side. My Grandma Hanson was even along for the outing, making it extra special.

Inspired by being out on the beach, surrounded by the people I loved, I decided it was time to attempt my first steps. It took me what seemed like forever to walk what was the equivalent of a block. Although I was frustrated, I just kept thinking, "I can walk.

This is going to work. I am going to *make this work*." I was determined—with each new step, my excitement grew.

I am happy and proud to say that, although my completion time went from three hours and forty-five minutes to four hours and twenty minutes, I was proud to be able to complete a full marathon with my dad about ten years after my accident. I now run with my dogs every morning—one of my favorite ways to get exercise and take time to mentally focus in on my day ahead.

Back To Life

It was a full six months until I returned to Los Angeles and was able to go back to work. And what a relief that was, as work has always been important to me. I can thank both my parents and their incredible work ethic for this.

In fact, when I woke up in the hospital after my accident, I apparently wrote in my notebook, asking someone to call my employer, Evans Furniture. One of my first instincts was to let them know that I wasn't going to work that day, to let them know what had happened, and to extend my apology. Of course, my family and friends responded with an incredulous, "Are you kidding us?"

Remarkably, six months after the accident, Evans Furniture once again gave me an inside sales job. What a company! I felt really blessed that they gave me an opportunity to come back. The position wasn't in the same location; however, it worked out really well. Within a short period of time, I was promoted to outside sales, which I enjoyed tremendously. That job was really my first taste of real collaboration and relationship building.

My Knight in Shining Armor?

Meanwhile, a lot had been developing in my personal life as well. After three years together, I married my boyfriend, Brian, who had faithfully stayed by my side during my recovery process. It was remarkable for a man so young to have the wherewithal to stay with me through the events of the accident and my recovery. Brian visited me on a daily basis throughout the entire process. He even took the summer off from UCLA and moved home with me to Arroyo Grande in order to take me to all my physical therapy appointments.

And I can tell you, I wasn't pretty—I basically looked like a smashed blueberry for a while. I was missing teeth, I had a bolt of sorts coming out of my head, and I had scars and bruises covering the majority of my body. Again, I couldn't get over how absolutely incredible it was for a young man, only 20 years old, to stick with me through all of this.

Although Brian and I had talked about the possibility of getting married, my mind wasn't focused on it. I really just wanted to get my life back to normal. I was always the one amongst my friends who would say, "I'm never going to get married. I'm going to travel the world and live adventurously!" However, when he continued to mention the idea, I couldn't help but think, "How could I *not* marry this guy?"

So, when Brian eventually did propose to me during a weekend cruise to Mexico, I knew that I couldn't I say "no." Of course, it didn't hurt that his proposal was like a scene out of the movie Titanic—before the ship sank of course. We were at the bow of the boat—on New Year's Eve, no less—chatting and drinking champagne. When the clock struck midnight, Brian gave me a huge kiss, slipped a ring on my finger and asked, "Will you marry me?" I just started bawling and said, "Yes." I remember thinking to myself, "If he behaved this amazingly under the horrible circumstances, he's a keeper...*right*?"

Wrong.

At first, Brian and I had a very loving relationship. He even had a wonderful family that I loved dearly. However, none of that could overcome the fact that Brian grew into a struggling artist who ultimately turned to binge drinking and beyond.

Brian always described a void he had inside of him that he was trying to fill. Because of this, he ended up having issues with depression. He's a true artist—very idealistic and very emotional—*very* different than me. I'm very black-and-white and levelheaded. Obviously, deep emotions makes for good art, but it can be seriously challenging in a marriage and quite frankly, I was too young to know this or figure it out at the time. Instead, I was a bit blinded by love and the Florence Nightingale effect.

Not Meant To Be...

At one point Brian and I talked about having children; however, I never quite felt ready. So, when I "accidentally" got pregnant, I couldn't ignore the nagging voice in the back of my mind: "Will this settle him [Brian] down? Will it get him to drink less and smoke less weed, and become a responsible adult?" Despite these thoughts, Brian and I became swept up in the excitement of it all. We were going to have a *baby*!

So we set up our first doctor's appointment, full of excitement and anticipation. The day of the appointment came. I can still remember how it felt, sitting in the examination room, listening to the doctor say, "I'm really sorry to have to tell you this, but there isn't a heartbeat."

What?

Brian and I were catapulted into an instant state of numbed shock. The doctor was able to show us the little shadowy image of our baby inside of me, but there wasn't a heartbeat. Within two days I went through the emotionally painful process of having it removed. Needless to say, that experience was like none other—I felt a lot of sadness for the physical and emotional loss, but also, ultimately, I felt (dare I say) a bit of relief. At this point, I was able to come to terms with how I honestly felt about the entire possibility of having a baby with Brian. I knew deep down in my heart that he wasn't the man that I wanted to have children with. Honestly, I wasn't even sure I wanted to have children at all.

You see, I think there are other ways to obtain the type of fulfillment that comes along with birthing a child. Seeing my mother adopt four kids helped me see this. I personally feel that I am better suited to give my time and energy to many, instead of just one or two. I've found that teaching and mentoring young women fulfills this part of me.

With the miscarriage behind us, our marriage came to an unceremonious halt six years in. Brian continued to struggle with each failing business endeavor, accompanied by his *cheating* on me ... not once, but *twice.* Supporting him in his struggle to gain a professional footing was one thing, but infidelity was where I drew the line. To add insult to injury, one of his cheating episodes involved a Mexican prostitute while on a drinking binge in Tijuana—I was irate! Although I agreed to try and work things out with him after he showed signs that he was a "changed man," his second romp in the hay with another woman was the literal "straw" that broke the marriage's back. I knew at that moment that I was done and our 10-year relationship was over.

This entire experience and the strength it took to bring it to a close was one of the defining moments of my personal reinvention. I began writing a book called *Thirty Reasons Not to Marry Before Thirty*. I was divorced at 30 while all of my girlfriends wisely put off marriage until after 30. They were the smart ones!

Lucky Breaks And... Layoffs

My personal life aside, there is also a very real—and at times raw—professional aspect to my reinvention. It's what I like to call my second "lucky" phase of life. It all started about two years out of school, when my first outside sales job with Evans Furniture afforded me the opportunity to start networking. It was at one of these business-networking events that I came upon my first opportunity to move into marketing.

During the course of a few networking lunches, I came to know a woman who was leaving her job at a high-tech recruiting firm. This was during the late 90s, and her job with the firm involved various aspects of marketing coordination. It was a hot market at the time, so she was moving on to start her own business. As we sat down to lunch one day, she reached out to me and said, "As you know, I'm leaving the firm and I'd like to recommend you for the job." I was elated—this was my lucky break! I was finally going to step into marketing, which is what I had always wanted to do.

After interviewing and landing the job, I spent my time diving into the world of HTML and general marketing practices. It was a small firm with about ten recruiters. I was learning a lot and I felt accomplished.

One day, only nine months into the position, my boss (the owner) called me into his office to tell me he had sold the company. When he told me I was being laid off, I immediately started tearing up. This was the first and only time I ever cried in an employer's office. This was my first break into marketing and here I was being cast aside. Furthermore, I had recently purchased a house while also financially supporting Brian's venture to launch a surfboard manufacturing and apparel company.

I soon realized that the sale of the company was the sole owner's meal ticket. He was done with the business and excited to sell. I, on the other hand, was devastated. I needed to find another J-O-B quickly!

Breast Cancer Scare

It was about this time that I'd recovered from what I thought would be my last surgery—a nerve transplant from the back of my leg to my left arm, to fill a quarter-millimeter gap in my radial nerve (which allows your wrist to flex up and down). The nerve had severed when my arm broke. I had to wait almost two years for the insurance company to approve the surgery. The claims department initially kicked it back as they said it was not "necessary."

With this very tricky procedure behind me I could focus on the task at hand—finding work. It was less than two weeks later that Brian noticed a lump in my left breast. It was astonishing that I hadn't felt it before, as it was well over the size of a golf ball. It's not like I had big boobs and it was hiding in the depths!

Of course your mind goes to the worst... could this be cancerous? After all of this, could I really have breast cancer? I was almost numb to the possibility.

I made yet another doctor appointment to have the mass biopsied. The three days I waited for the results seemed like an eternity. I couldn't sleep. I couldn't eat. I remember thinking, "How could God get me all this way and then let this happen?" Well, it didn't happen. The tumor was found to be benign and I quickly had it removed. With that behind me, I returned to the task of finding a J-O-B.

First Taste of Collaboration

After three months of searching I was able to land a good job at a full-service marketing agency. Part of the firm created marketing collateral like brochures, menus, and other printed materials. The other arm of the firm worked with promotional marketing items like pens, water bottles, and anything branded. They also started to move into web development work, creating company websites and online stores. We worked with clients such as DIRECTV Sports, Sun America, Fox News Channel, and Epson.

Although I started out as an Account Coordinator, I quickly moved up to an Account Director position, where I was making about $80,000 a year. My position grew into a role where I helped manage collaboration projects between companies like DIRECTV Sports and large retail merchandisers.

Being in my mid-20s I thought I had died and gone to heaven! I was working with large, well-known companies, and I was earning more money than I ever imagined possible at my age. I even had my own assistant! I was truly at the height of feeling professionally "lucky."

In usual form, I decided that I didn't have enough to do, so I pursued my MBA. I went through two years of night school at California State University, Dominguez Hills, with the long-term vision of moving up the corporate ladder.

Right around this time, I also started seeing trouble brewing at the firm. It was owned and run by two cousins and a third partner, Roger, who made it his business to stop by my office daily and ask me when I was going to run away with him to Turks and Caicos. We were both married but that certainly didn't stop his advances. This ritual began to wear on me, but at the time I had no idea what to do. I was the only female at this level in the company and I felt my job would be at stake if I said anything.

The company lost a few key accounts and the cousins started having visible arguments about the business, making it clear that things were not going well for the company. Ultimately—you guessed it—they closed the business and I was *laid off* yet again!

Brian and I had been talking for a while about the possibility of moving back to San Diego, so I decided to focus on completing my MBA by finishing all of the 22 remaining credits in one semester. I also worked as a teaching assistant and took on other paid research work to make ends meet.

With diploma in hand we quickly sold our house and got the heck out of Los Angeles. It was fun in my early twenties but the traffic and the overall fast-pace was wearing on both of us. As was reminiscent to my prior job search in San Diego, my prospects were meager. It was 2001 and the economy was wounded. I started reaching out to my San Diego network, hoping my recent

MBA would help me land a job that would take my career to the next level. I was certainly not expecting what came next...

My Stint With The Mexican Mafia

While chatting with my dad over the phone one day, he said, "You know Todd, the pastor's son? Well, he's now also living in San Diego and I heard he's doing pretty well. You should connect with him."

It's funny how memories can come flooding back at the mere mention of a name. I vividly remember Todd from my childhood. He was about five years older than me. I can still picture him in all of his "goth" glory—he was one of the "cool kids" in my childhood book. I remember my inner dialogue even now as an adult: "Oh my gosh, I'm going to call Todd Pitcher... *wow*!"

As it turned out, Todd was working for an investment firm in the elegant Symphony Towers building, located in downtown San Diego. Walking into his offices on the 20th floor of the building, I was immediately enveloped by the richness of it all—corner offices were outfitted with mahogany furniture and 360-degree views of the San Diego Bay. It was truly breathtaking.

I spent some time getting up to speed on Todd's career and family life, when the founder of the company stopped by to introduce himself. After a few minutes of pleasantries and general introductory chit-chat he said, "So, you have some marketing experience... some of our clients are high-net-worth individuals who need marketing for their companies. My friend's cousin's kid is a graphic designer and I was thinking of bringing him onto the team. How would you like to spearhead our new marketing division?"

Had my "lucky" streak returned?

"... Oh, and by the way, we're going to pay you under the table." Okay, well, perhaps he didn't immediately put that part in that direct terminology, but you get the idea. Having grown up in a small business environment, I was not a complete stranger to people being paid under the table (shhh … don't tell the IRS.) I was still a little hesitant, but in the end, having been unemployed for eight months won out.

I started off with a salary of $40,000 a year. My earnings had literally been cut in half, but it's also important to remember that this was 2001, right after the dot-com crash, and things were going a little haywire in the market.

I really needed a job. And it was an interesting opportunity to spearhead a marketing division. I thought, "Why not? I'm going to give this a go." So I got my fancy corner office with a mahogany desk (cool!) and started working with the graphic design team to put together programs and other collateral.

Then September 11th happened. I vividly remember the call from my neighbor, as I was getting ready to head out the front door, telling me to turn on the television. I sat there watching the events of the morning in utter disbelief. It was for me, as it was for many others, an important reminder of how lucky we are to be alive.

Longing To Give Back

When we finally did return to work two days later, everyone came back with a renewed sense of humanity, wanting to pitch in and help the affected families in some way. As a result, the CEO asked the newly formed "marketing division" to put together an event, which we ended up naming the "Proud to Be an American Expo." The goal was to quickly raise money for the families and victims of this tragedy. However, underlying all of this was a sense of "hey, there's a way to profit from this" from the executive team. This gave me an uneasy feeling, but I tried not to pay too much attention to it. This was my chance to make a difference!

The entire team (or so I thought) and I put our best efforts forward to plan and produce a successful event. At first it appeared everything was moving along exceptionally well. One of our team members (Art), who was responsible for obtaining sponsorships, announced 12 weeks before the event that he had secured a large, well-known corporate donor, Gateway Computers, who pledged $50,000. With that one "big-name" backer and a handful of other small sponsors, we had what we needed to plan and hold a successful event. At this juncture we began engaging vendors, hiring musicians, and even secured a local skateboard company to set up a half-pipe. This event was really going to be something!

A few days before the actual event, it came to light that the large corporate sponsor we were banking on was not giving us the $50,000. When Art was pressed for details and for the money, he kept stalling, saying the sponsorship was going through the proper "channels." Whatever his motive for lying, it became evident that the sponsor never intended to provide any large-scale backing whatsoever.

We were forced to go ahead with the event with only small sums of money backing us to cover all of the hard costs. We were definitely operating at a loss at this point. Even with this, we pressed on and delivered the event, and the participants were none the wiser. This was, however, the beginning of the end.

We all knew the ship was going down. Besides this latest debacle, we had already started to see less frequent paychecks and could sense there were some other unsavory things going on in the business. The day after the event was over, the two graphic designers and I promptly cut our losses and quit.

Soon after leaving the company, I learned that the owner was somehow tied to members of the Mexican Mafia, managing the investments of some of the individuals high up in the organization in Mexico City. I don't know the exact details, but the rumors were he was embezzling money from them. This, along with who knows what other shady dealings, ultimately landed him in jail for a very long time. So this was what I like to call "my six-month stint working for the Mexican Mafia!"

Getting A Real Job

After that experience (as you can imagine), I put all of my focus on looking for and securing a credible, legitimate job. I initially landed an inside marketing position with a biotech firm. However, I kept looking, since the position wasn't a great long-term fit for me.

Soon thereafter, I came across a Director of Marketing position for a company called Infogate. It was a long shot, but luckily they were looking for a couple of things that I could offer: 1) client interfacing marketing experience, and 2) an MBA. I interviewed with Cliff Boro, the CEO and a well-known entrepreneur in San Diego, and got the job. What a relief. I guess that MBA was finally paying off!

I was excited at the opportunity to work at Infogate, as they were a company ahead of their time. When I joined the startup, they were in the process of transitioning from a free, ad-supported model for their technical resources to a paid subscription model. The system worked similarly to modern-day Google Alerts. When specific keywords were entered into the system, it would pull from the 2,000 or so news sources to generate and deliver a comprehensive stream of the latest industry-specific information to one's desktop, via a TV-style ticker. This provided our clients with an extremely effective way to follow their competition, along with staying up to date on breaking news in their industry. This allowed our partners, like CNN, the LA Times, and USA Today to better monetize their web traffic.

The good news was that Infogate was backed by a good amount of venture capital. However, the bad news was the company's burn rate (the rate at which they were spending that capital) was extremely high—this "show" wasn't going to go on much longer. They either needed to raise more money—above the $30 million they had already raised—or sell. Unfortunately, I wasn't surprised when I did, in fact, start to hear the murmurs throughout the office. I worked there just under two years when America Online (AOL) bought the company, officially and squarely landing me in *layoff number three* by age 30! (Of course not counting the mafia incident.)

The Pinnacle Of Reinvention

At this point, I reached the peak of my reinvention—it was time to control my own destiny from start to finish. I had a couple options at this point. I could find another J-O-B (which to me seemed like a death sentence), or I could create my own business. Going back to work for another company where I had no control over how they chose to do business, how or to whom they sold their products, how they raised money, or what direction they chose to take their business in was no longer an option. From this point, moving forward, I was going to be in the driver's seat!

After having been the breadwinner for my married life, I felt it was my turn to follow in my father's footsteps. Plus, San Diego is small businesses town. I felt my chance of success was just as high (if not higher) creating my own J-O-B than it would be going to work for another company that could be bought, sold, or downsized. Now I would be creating my own world, my own environment, my own experience.

There were many points throughout this endeavor when I felt like I was in over my head, but my experience and recent education gave me the confidence to take the "fake it 'til you make it" attitude—an attitude I have routinely applied throughout my career. My mantra is, "Say *yes* and Google it!"

A Lucky Life...

Throughout my 20s I went about life, making my way along the corporate path, always thinking that I would somehow get that little nudge or acquire that little bit of additional education that would lead to getting paid more and "success." Unfortunately, I didn't learn these skills in school or at home, nor did I have any effective role models along the way to help me navigate corporate culture. As a result, I never learned how to negotiate or how to fight to get ahead.

Although I never worked for a monolithic *corporation*, I've certainly experienced my fair share of *corporate culture* and have been privy to the "herd" or "sheep" mentality that runs rampant. I can still vividly recall what it felt like to experience the injustice of people being treated unfairly and, more specifically, seeing women not getting raises or promotions as readily as men.

One of those vivid memories involved a male Account Manager who was a counterpart of mine at the marketing agency where I worked. One day he walked into the co-founder's office and stated, straight out, "I want your job." As I found out through a conversation with him later, the co-founder wasn't at all taken aback. In fact, he had responded with a supportive, "I respect that!" To top that off, he was given a raise because he had the moxie to step up and ask how he could continue to climb the ladder. This *never* would have occurred to me!

Experiences like this, along with many others, continually made me feel like I was just part of the herd mentality, caught up in the wheelhouse of "getting ahead." We learn young to follow the rules, do what we're told (so to speak), and constantly work towards receiving a stellar review so that we can get that "3 percent raise." Why else do we work but to earn money, *right*? What about *passion*?

I don't know about you, but passion wasn't acknowledged or talked about while I was working in the corporate world, and frankly, it's not really practical for many people. Who has the luxury to focus on passion when we all have obligations? Personally, I had spent most of my professional life, up until then, supporting my husband and all of his ventures. There wasn't time for me to really dive in and figure out what I was passionate about. I didn't hate what I was doing, but I certainly wasn't passionate about it.

That's why, to this day, I say I feel lucky—and I truly mean I feel lucky—that I was literally shoved off the J-O-B cliff and given no other choice but to take control of my own professional destiny. In fact, I don't feel that people who continually work to climb the proverbial "ladder of success" are as lucky!

Yes, that's what I said—people who are climbing the ladder to success aren't as *lucky*, and here's why.

Buying into the concept that success is defined by advancing in a company, getting a new car and a bigger house, taking a vacation, and buying more "stuff" is, in my humble opinion, a trap that is easy to fall into. Our "more is better" culture is extremely pervasive in corporate America.

What I'm advocating is to think differently. Don't place such a high value on *stuff.* Instead, learn to live with less. Being an entrepreneur is the most liberating, amazing experience. Lucky for me, I didn't grow up with much, so simplifying was not as difficult for me as it may be for others.

Why don't you give it a try?

Take a moment to step back from your life and visually rise above it, floating over all of the "stuff" that collectively makes up your day-to-day existence. Now, try to look at it from a different perspective: one that asks, "Do I truly need all of this? What's really going to make me happy?"

The truth, as countless studies have suggested, is that happiness doesn't come from buying new things or making more money. In fact, a well-known study conducted by Dr. Ryan T. Howell, an associate professor of psychology at San Francisco State University (Howell & Howell 2008), revealed that after a person's basic needs are met (i.e., food, shelter, etc.), the relationship between income and happiness is negligible. So, you may find, as I did, that the things that truly bring you happiness have nothing to do with money.

It's true, going after your passion may result in your having to cut down on your consumption of "stuff", and you may have to live with less and change your life in other ways, but that's probably a good thing. And if you have children this is a unique opportunity to teach them these lessons from an early age.

More importantly, stepping off that treadmill and shifting your perspective towards being in control of your life choices, as I did, will put you well on your way towards controlling your own destiny. I can't blame anyone else for anything that's happened in my life—not my divorce, not my layoffs, not my car accident—nothing. I don't hold anyone but myself accountable for choices I've made or will make moving forward. This alone is incredibly empowering and liberating.

Chapter 3
Liberation

HAVING EXPERIENCED A HEFTY dose of bad leadership first-hand, I decided it was time to learn the "right" leadership style. With that, I launched myself into exploring several leadership programs offered in the San Diego community. Through my research I came to rest on a particular approach that really resonated with me: servant leadership.

Although servant leadership can be found in many religious texts, the philosophy itself transcends any particular religious tradition. In fact, it's such an ancient philosophy that it is said to have existed long before the teachings of the Bible. For example, there are passages that relate to servant leadership in the *Tao Te Ching*, a classic Chinese text attributed to philosopher and poet Lao Tzu, who is believed to have lived in China sometime between 570 BCE and 490 BCE.

It was Robert K. Greenleaf who founded the modern servant leadership movement. In his essay, "The Servant Leader", first published in 1970, he says:

> *"It begins with the natural feeling that one wants to serve first. Then conscious choice brings one to aspire to lead. That person is sharply different from one who is leader first, perhaps because of the need to assuage an unusual power drive or to acquire material possessions ... The leader-first and the servant-first are two extreme types. Between them there are shadings and blends that are part of the infinite variety of human nature."*

He goes on to explain:

> *"The difference manifests itself in the care taken by the servant-first to make sure that other people's highest priority needs are being served. The best test, and difficult to administer, is: Do those served grow as persons? Do they, while being served, become healthier, wiser, freer, more autonomous, more likely themselves to become servants? And what is the effect on the least privileged in society? Will they benefit or at least not be further deprived?"*

Healthier, wiser, freer … this definitely resonated with me!

I immediately enrolled in a nine-month training program on servant leadership, hoping to define my leadership style as well as meet new people. I did indeed achieve both! This new perspective on leadership and working with people through a lens of "service" helped me tap back into my true spirit. I gained confidence, knowing I had the power to truly help others.

Using My Perspective

It was with this resolve and focus that I started my marketing-strategy consulting firm. I named my business "Perspective Marketing", as I felt I could help small businesses see issues from an objective angle. Over an eight-year period, my niche emerged: helping small, service-based companies grow through relationship marketing. Of course, I took a large pay cut. It took me several years to get close to the salary I was earning in my last J-O-B, but it was worth it. I had freedom and was in control of my destiny.

For additional financial stability, I also decided to see if I could pick up a part-time teaching job. Through a series of connections back in my MBA program, Cal State University, Dominguez Hills offered me an adjunct teaching position in marketing for one of their online programs. Soon thereafter, I was fortunate enough to meet the Director of Education for the Fashion Institute of Design and Merchandising (FIDM) at an event. After sharing a bit about my experience in Brian's surf apparel business, she asked if I would ever consider teaching. After a bit of contemplation I agreed! I taught a couple of Marketing and Entrepreneurship classes each quarter. The eight years I spent at FIDM provided the stability I needed to generate extra income and provided an extra boost while I launched my business. I especially enjoyed teaching young women at FIDM. It was as if all of the actions and steps I had taken up to that point were finally coming together and making sense.

Growing My Network

I quickly realized that "networking" - going to industry events and meeting potential clients and collaborators - was an important part of building a business. In 2006 I met a talented attorney from Texas, Linda Lattimore, just as she was in the early stages of launching a professional organization, Women's Global Network (WGN). WGN's mission was to build local business connections, while helping women in developing nations launch small businesses through micro-loans.

I liked Linda immediately. She had such a warm, welcoming way about her. I consider her one of my true mentors along my entrepreneurial path. (I will go into more detail on this in the next section of the book.)

A little over two years after launching WGN, Linda transitioned back to Texas for work. She asked me to take over the San Diego chapter, and although I was a little nervous about my ability to lead such a wonderful, accomplished group of women, I accepted the nomination! Over the next two years, running WGN gave me not only great servant leadership experience but also good visibility. It catapulted me into many new opportunities and built my confidence greatly.

My next adventure on this collaborative path arose out of my love for fashion. My affiliation with the Fashion Institute led me to launch a fashion networking organization and several non-profit projects, including a venture with the San Diego Visual Arts Network called "Art Meets Fashion." This was a unique collaboration project, pairing visual artists and fashion designers throughout San Diego. In addition to the artist and designer duo, each team also included a documenter (photographer or videographer) and educator. The goal was to document the creative process between artist and designer. The educator would then take the learnings back into San Diego high schools in order to inspire teens to explore a career in the arts. The work was showcased at the San Diego International Airport and was also displayed at various galleries and boutiques. This successful and inspiring venture bolstered my drive to collaborate!

Incubating New Business Ideas

After leading WGN for two years, I had the opportunity to step into a temporary leadership position with Ladies Who Launch (LWL). I took over management of the local chapter in August 2009. This provided me with the opportunity to work with a new group of entrepreneurial women and with a national organization that had fairly good brand recognition. I thoroughly enjoyed leading LWL's Incubator Intensive Workshops, which were equal parts inspiration, education, and accountability for six to eight female entrepreneurs. Over the course of the two years I had the pleasure of working with over 200 women in the launch of their business.

Taking this concept of collaboration to the next level, I decided to join forces with a local business woman, Michelle Bergquist, founder of Connected Women of Influence, to launch the "Business Women's Mega Mixer" in 2010. As a showcase of professional women's organizations, the Mega Mixer provided businesswomen throughout San Diego County with an opportunity to gain a broader professional perspective by cross-pollinating with hundreds of other like-minded women. What a success it was—the first event drew more than 25 organizations and 500 women, and raised thousands of dollars for the Women's History Museum.

It was at this point that I truly realized that I had reached my peak potential as a freelancing "jack of all trades". Although everything was going well, it was going in way too many directions. I finally realized that I was pretty burned out and needed to create a business that was bigger than myself—something I could scale!

> *"Everyone that starts a business is a technician that suffers from an Entrepreneurship seizure. Small businesses do not work the way they are intended because the technician only works in the business and cannot also have the foresight to work on the business at the same time."*
>
> ***Michael Gerber, the E-Myth.***

Hera Hub is Born!

Hera Hub really grew out of need. It was a need that I identified within myself and, as I was coming to realize, was a common plight for many entrepreneurial women. I had spent the last eight years working from home and, while it was convenient and cost-effective as a small, service-based business, it definitely had its downfalls. I was finding it too distracting and isolating to continue working from home. The laundry and dishes would nag at me, the dogs would whine to be taken on a run, and the doorbell would intermittently ring with a new delivery or someone trying to sell me something. *Anything* had the power to take my attention away from what I *needed* to be doing!

Privacy and the desire to appear professional were also major concerns. This daytime challenge was coupled with the struggle to find evening event space for my networking groups. Hotels and private rooms were always too expensive, and community centers and libraries were closing left and right. Then, one night in 2010, I was turned on to the concept of "coworking" while hosting a networking event at San Diego's first coworking space, the Hive Haus. The idea was hatched!

Over the next six months, I dove into market research and visited coworking spaces in New York, Los Angeles, and San Francisco in order to get a sense of what was out there. One thing became crystal clear... there was a gap in the market. Most of the spaces I visited were either messy and loud (sort of looked like fraternity houses) or cold and quiet. Neither of these environments spoke to my market or me. There was only one other female-focused workspace out there, and it was all the way in New York City.

Old White Men

When I first launched into securing the physical space for Hera Hub, little did I know that I was lining up for one of my biggest challenges—the commercial real estate process! Negotiating a lease was much more complex and challenging than I had ever imagined. I had two strikes against me - new business and new concept. No one was willing to take a risk. To top off the experience, I was "patted on the head" by older men in this very traditional industry more times than I care to recall. I could almost see them thinking, "oh isn't that cute... these little ladies want their own space."

I spent three months negotiating my first deal directly with a building owner who was interested in the coworking model. I figured that I could get by without a broker and just use a real estate attorney. That blew up in the 11th hour when he decided to launch his own coworking space—*after* I'd shared my extensive business plan and all my financials. Then history repeated itself (although this time I was armed with a broker) when negotiating my second deal. We made it to the point where I was in the process of obtaining a cashier's check for the deposit and first month's rent, only to have the building owner tell me that he had found a better fit for the space. Six months wasted!

I was devastated. I remember thinking, "Maybe it isn't meant to be, after all!"

As fate would have it, my third lease negotiation also got off to a rocky start. After submitting my proposal, I found out the building was in escrow. My heart sank. I couldn't keep this up much longer as I was already heavily marketing the concept to my community. Every day people were asking, "When are you opening?"

After waiting four weeks for the new owner to respond, we finally had a chance to meet. Much to my delight, they knew about the coworking model and had visited the Hive Haus. Finally, someone who "gets it!"

Just after beginning the negotiation process on an open ground-floor space (approximately 3,700 square feet) they received a another bid from an existing tenant in an adjacent suite. All I can remember is thinking, "Seriously? I'm doomed!"

To my relief, the building owners came back with a suggestion to look at a suite in the sister building. The space was more than 8,000 square feet, which they agreed could be split. With a little vision, I sectioned off close to 5,000 square feet and put in a new proposal. It was a big risk, as it was quite a bit larger than the prior spaces. We pressed on with the back-forth process.

Ready, Fire, Aim

Because of what had happened in the prior two deals I kept looking for other space while we continued to negotiate. I learned first-hand that nothing is final until I had the keys in-hand.

I had recently read a book by Michael Masterson (*Ready, Fire, Aim: Zero to $100 Million in No Time Flat*), which gave me the drive to try a different tactic. In early April 2011, I met Amy Mewborn, the recent franchisee for Xtend Barre (a popular form of ballet-meets-Pilates.) She overheard me lamenting about the commercial real estate industry at a WGN networking event. She mentioned her newly launched location, which was not far from where

I was looking to land, and invited me to take a look at her second studio, which she wasn't yet utilizing.

I showed up at 9am the next morning to tour the 700-square-foot space, which happened to boast dark brown hardwood floors and aqua-colored walls—pretty much Hera Hub colors. I wrote her a check on the spot for a temporary lease. Within one week we had the IKEA furniture and ambiance in place. We even set up a makeshift meeting room in a storage space. We made it work!

Let me take a moment to explain what I mean by ambiance. I'm a Libra so my surroundings are important to me. I like balance and order. It's important that a space "feel" just right. Even my home office was carefully set up with accessories that made it not only feel warm and welcoming but also productive. This was inclusive of running water, scented candles, ample natural light, and ambient music. I had the instinct for placement of these things well before I knew what Feng Shui was. When I set up the temporary location I applied the same principles. If I was going to convince someone to come work in a fitness studio it had better "feel" right!

A few weeks after opening a visitor and commented, "It feels like a spa in here." Aha, that was it! So I coined the phrase "spa-inspired workspace!"

I officially opened the "temporary" Hera Hub on tax day, April 15, 2011 - just a little over a year from idea to doors open. Despite the mirrored walls and the intermittent sounds of women groaning through leg-lifts in the next room, I was able to create a space for collaboration and inspiration. It was finally coming together!

Taking Flight

Knowing I was in the final stretch bolstered my faith and resolve—Hera Hub was going to take flight! I continued the negotiation process while running the temporary space. I was elated when we finally came to an agreement. Despite the roadblocks, my dream was becoming a reality. We finished construction in early August, and I officially opened the doors on Monday, August 15, 2011.

I truly feel everything I've done in my life led up to the moment I launched Hera Hub. It is a natural extension of the collaboration I have fostered throughout my entire career. It has taken a lot of 80-hour workweeks, but I'm proud to say Hera Hub has positively affected the lives of thousands of women, and a few good men! We grew to more than 100 members in the first year and launched our second and third locations in San Diego County to respond to the demand. In May 2015 we launched our first brand extension in Washington DC and are on a path to open many more in the upcoming years!

What Is Hera Hub?

So, those of you not yet "in the know" may be wondering, "Just what is Hera Hub?" Hera Hub is a shared, flexible work and meeting space where entrepreneurial women can create and collaborate in a professional, productive, spa-like environment. The platform provides our members with connections to other business experts, access to educational workshops, and visibility within the community, thus giving them the support they need to be prosperous.

Unlike other coworking spaces that tend to focus on recreating typical office settings, the Hera Hub locations were designed to benefit all five senses.

1. Sight – beautiful art, live plants, calming colors, and friendly faces.

2. Smell – aromatic candles that relax and invigorate.

3. Sound – soft, spa-like music and tranquil running water.

4. Feel – Feng Shui incorporated to ensure the space is effective and productive.

5. Taste – fresh-brewed coffee, tea, spa water, and healthy snacks.

I've never really allowed myself to claim my creativity until launching Hera Hub. This business has allowed me to explore this aspect of myself, as I've never done before. It's not only the décor, but also the programming and events. I've never had so much fun in my entire life.

Yes, I've built a bit of a "club". I allowed myself to go big and put every intention and resource into one business. I've been able to attract the most amazing women to the community and have built something that most only dream of—a beautiful, welcoming, relaxing yet vibrant space where women connect, collaborate, and flourish. I've created my own utopia, and perhaps Hera Hub will be where you discover yours!

Who Was Hera?

Significant thought went into developing Hera Hub's name and logo. Hera, the Greek goddess of women, was revered as the only goddess who accompanied a woman through every step of her life—blessing and protecting her family and financial security. Hera represents the fullness of life and affirms that women can use their wisdom in the pursuit of any goal they choose.

Remarkably, the beautiful male peacock feather is her symbol. Perhaps I already knew my life's quest when I started selling Mr. Peabody's feathers at age eight!

Why Women?

I truly believe that women interact differently and are instinctively more collaborative in their approach to business. I felt it was important to create a space that was beautiful, comfortable, and feminine yet also very professional.

Many women running small businesses also have to juggle family life and therefore feel an affinity with other women in the same situation. A supportive environment where women feel they easily relate to others helps get to that point in the relationship where they know, like, and trust the other person and are therefore more likely to ask for feedback or refer business.

My Personal Flight

Looking back over the past 40 years of my life, I can safely say that everything I experienced—the good and the bad—led me to where I am today and will continue to propel me forward.

My childhood taught me to recognize and utilize the resources available to me, to work hard, and to try my best. From my father, I learned to be persistent, resilient, and compassionate. My mother instilled the importance of creativity and trusting my gut.

My accident taught me to really value my health and family and to live life to the fullest. Knowing that things can change in the blink of an eye makes me more mindful of living every day fully and utilizing everything life has to offer.

Making the jump from employee to entrepreneur was both challenging and exhilarating. Down deep I knew pursuing my dream was a much better idea than relying on someone else's ability to provide me with a steady J-O-B. Call me crazy, but I also chose to see the 2008 stock-market crash as an eye-opening gift. My stock portfolio (like everyone else's) took about a 40-percent dip. While launching Hera Hub was a risk—I invested close to $60,000 of my own money and borrowed an additional $30,000 from my father—I felt like I was at least "in control" of the outcome, whereas I felt I had *no* control leaving the money in mutual funds with companies I didn't even keep track of. Succeed or fail, at least I knew I was in the driver's seat.

I also learned that in order to be my best, I can't say "yes" to every opportunity that presents itself. I now understand the importance of being deliberate when making choices—to avoid becoming distracted by projects, objects, or commitments that can pull me away from my long-term goals.

Surviving the accident and the end of my marriage taught me that I could recover from anything and that what doesn't kill you can truly make you stronger. Through each change, I learned that reinvention is an important part of life, and being willing to redefine my personal goals and professional life was absolutely necessary for not only my survival, but also my success. Starting my own business after all of my job losses and seemingly overwhelming challenges has solidified my belief—I am in control of my own destiny. I am in control of my own *flight*.

Why Flight Club?

I vividly remember going to see the movie *Fight Club* with my ex-husband, Brian, the week after it came out in the fall of 1999. I've always been a Brad Pitt fan (most women are), and Brian was a fan of dark gritty movies, which I grew to appreciate. Our VHS collection boasted movies like "Reservoir Dogs" and "Pulp Fiction".

What struck me about this film, besides the fact the Brad Pitt has his shirt off for most of the movie, was the plot: Edward Norton works in a sea of gray, drab cubicles and is bored with his mundane life. As he says in the movie, "Everything is a copy of a copy." Norton is drawn to Pitt because of what he proposes: starting an underground club for those who want to break out of the norm and really "feel" something. This is just what he needs to cure his pathetic life.

This was about the same time I was contemplating "leaning out" of my own gray cubicle and exploring new territory. I was intrigued. I was ready to ditch the "move up the ladder" mentality.

As I mentioned previously, I had the privilege to lead my own "clubs"—Women's Global Network and Ladies Who Launch—giving others a chance to break of out of the day-to-day monotony, get something off the ground, and connect with a bigger purpose. Hera Hub is now also something that gets referred to as a "club" from time to time. The connotation of "belonging" is a powerful one.

I've always loved flying—not only the feeling of flying, but also the doors that it opens. I love, love, love to travel. So far, I've been to 22 countries and have another 80-plus on my list. I've often applied the analogy of "taking flight" to launching a business. The idea of getting something off the ground and soaring is a strong visual for me.

At its very core, Flight Club reflects the essence of the peacocks and other birds that I grew up with. The male peacock is the symbol of the Greek goddess Hera, as she was known for her big beautiful eyes (like those in the peacock feather) and for being watchful over women at every stage of their lives. The very intention behind Hera Hub is to support women like you—the women who make up our Flight Club—as you launch your dream businesses.

The First Flight Club

Since I launched Hera Hub in 2011, I always envisioned taking a group of women on an exotic retreat to help them launch their businesses. That opportunity came to me when an East Coast-based company, Learning Through Travel, approached me about planning a trip to Greece and walking in the footsteps of Hera. I immediately said "yes", and we began planning.

The inaugural Flight Club took place in October 2015. Six women and I walked in the footsteps of the incredible Greek gods and goddesses, including Hera and Zeus. We visited all the major archaeological sites in Athens, Nafplio, Delphi, Epidaurus, Olympia, and Mycenae. In between stops, I worked with these amazing women to map out the foundations of their businesses and set a path for future growth. We also sailed the Aegean Sea to the beautiful islands of Santorini, Crete, Patmos, Rhodes, Mykonos, as well as visiting the historical site of Ephesus in Turkey. For me, Rhodes and Santorini were particularly special, as there I was reminded of what it means to embrace my adventurous soul and fully experience life.

By the end of the trip, each woman had a solid plan for future growth, knowing exactly what she needed to do get her business off the ground. Upon our return, she had the support of the Hera Hub community to keep her on track. And so went the first of many Flight Club adventures.

First Flight Club in front of Temple of Hera at Olympia

The Flight Has Just Begun…

Now that you've heard my story, the next step is to map our your flight path. In the next section we will take you through a journey of self discovery and, hopefully, help you identify your dream business.

Part Two: Planning Your Flight to Freedom

Chapter 4 Finding Your Path

I'M SO EXCITED TO share stories and guidance of six amazing female leaders, as well as the "lean out" moments of eight inspiring women. You can learn more about these women through one-on-one video interviews at www.FlightClubBook.com.

Here we dive into the five linchpins of launching a thriving venture—each complete with an exercise to help you find your path.

So, I encourage you to buy a special notebook to document your intentions, grab your favorite pen, and get ready to dive into:

Mindset

Fear

Passion

Strengths

Vision

Why Do Women "Lean Out"?

While everyone talks about the work/life balance equation as the driving force for women to launch a business, a study released by the National Association of Women Business Owners reveals that, while this is one source of motivation for 65 percent of women, the biggest reason (for 92 percent), is the ability to do something they are passionate about. This is closely followed by the ability to be in charge of one's decisions and the potential for higher earning power.

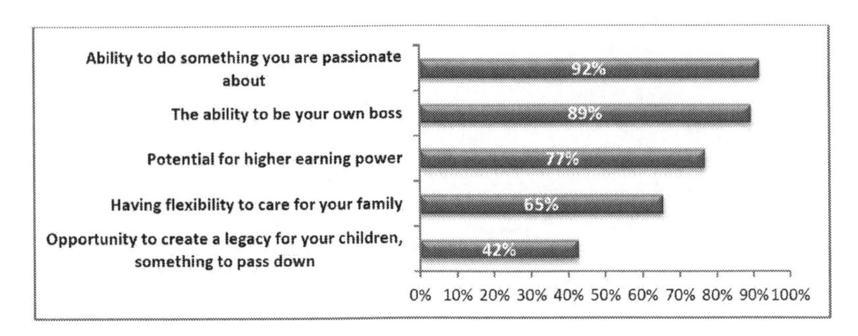

For most women, work/life balance doesn't mean they work less. In fact, most entrepreneurs actually work more than employees do. What matters most is that they are in control of their time. They decide when they work, where they work, and how they work.

Changing Landscapes

We are told from an early age that the "good life" follows a certain pattern: education, J-O-B, house, marriage, kids, college fund, pension, and retirement. The problem with this sequential path is that it doesn't necessarily work out that way anymore.

Let's start with education. More families are finding that college expenses are unaffordable. Some students are graduating with debt in excess of $100,000, putting home ownership (step #3) out of their reach any time before they're 40!

If past generations dreamed of the prestige and perks that come with a corner office, the dream of the millennial generation (also known as Generation Y) appears significantly different. A Bentley University survey of millennials found that 66 percent of respondents have a desire to start their own businesses. Driven in part by both the recent recession and an overall shift in thinking, some are calling them this group the "gig" generation—freelancing, picking up odd jobs, or driving for Uber versus getting a traditional 9-to-5 J-O-B. Only 13 percent of survey respondents said their career goal involves climbing the corporate ladder to become a CEO or president.

If you think about it, the 2008 crash forced many of us to create our own jobs (necessity entrepreneurship). The lack of opportunity actually birthed more freedom, more risk-taking, and more ambition because many had no other choice.

Fred Tuffile, director of Bentley's Entrepreneurial Studies program, says that millennials are eager to make their own pathways because they suspect the traditional ones may lead nowhere. "Millennials see chaos, distrust of management, breaking of contracts, and bad news associated with business," he says. "They've watched their relatives get fired and their peers sit in cubicles and they think, 'There has to be a better way.' Millennials are realizing that starting a company, even if it crashes and burns, teaches them more in two years than sitting in a cubicle for 20 years," Tuffile says. "While they know their chances of creating another Facebook are low, they do think it's fairly easy to create a cool startup."

As one Hera Hub millennial member puts it: "I don't want to go work for 'The Man.' I feel compelled to do work I'm passionate about … work that has meaning. Sitting in a cubicle sounds like a death sentence to me."

LEAN OUT MOMENT

Judi Bonilla

I remember that "a-ha!" moment well. I had been working for CEVA Logistics for close to five years. It was a good job with a solid company. I had just finished an audit and was working away at my desk when I overheard some coworkers talking. I remember thinking, "These are not my people," and more importantly, a feeling that "this" was not for me. I almost said out loud, "There is more for me than this." I didn't know what that "more" was, but it set me on a mission to figure it out.

The journey actually started years before with two major life experiences. The first was my mother's sudden passing. It was a painful and difficult time for my family. From that experience, I knew I wanted something better for my friends and their parents.

The second was living overseas and observing the lives of older adults in other cultures. There, I learned there was an opportunity for a different approach to aging. As I began my research on the business of aging, there was still a fair amount of doubt in my mind that I could make this new career path work. As someone once said, "Although it may be a good idea, it doesn't mean it's a business." At age 48, I took the leap and went back to school to become a gerontologist.

I knew the trajectory was going to be long. Funny enough, I felt like I was on my own personal Apollo mission, trying to hit the arc of the market at the right time. It's been ten years since I made the decision to "bet on me first," and I've never looked back!

ABOUT

Gerontologist | Lifestyle Aging Expert | Social Entrepreneur

Judi is the founder of Advocates for Aging, which creates interactive educational programs. The basis of her innovative system is her belief that livable communities are built by linking people to programs and services to improve their quality of their life. Her motto: Educate - Inspire - Empower.

www.JudiBonilla.com

Encorepreneurs

Millennials are not the only group driving entrepreneurial growth. The 55+ market (sometimes called encorepreneurs) is rapidly turning to business ownership.

According to the Kauffman Index of Entrepreneurial Activity, the share of entrepreneurs in the 55–64 age group jumped from 14.3 percent in 1996 to 23.4 percent in 2012. The stats also show that experience drives success: a study by the Kauffman Foundation showed that people over 55 are almost twice as likely to found successful companies as those between the ages of 20 and 34.

Whether you're in your twenties, over fifty, or somewhere in between, this might be the right time to "lean out" and start-up.

23 signs that you may be ready to start your own business:

1. *You feel stuck. You've hit a wall and are no longer fulfilled by your job.*

2. *The light bulb came on and stayed on. One day you're in your kitchen, or more likely the shower, and you conjure up an unmet need. You keep working it over in your mind and even start obsessing about it. You can't let it go!*

3. *You're passionate. It's not just a good idea; it's what you feel you were put on this earth to do! You start to tell everyone you know—even your mother-in-law! You want to build your dream!*

4. *You're independent. You would rather blaze your own trail rather than following the herd. You've always been the*

girl that zigged when others zagged.

5. *You're motivated. You're willing to work nights and weekends on your idea.*

6. *You're disciplined. You're the one who follows through with your New Year's resolutions through 12/31.*

7. *You're organized. You color code your calendar - every color has meaning!*

8. *You feel a need to help people. This desire to help people enhance their lives can keep you going during the highs and lows of running an operation.*

9. *You are determined. Let's say you have an idea but everyone is telling you it can't be done. What are you going to do about this situation? This experience might be motivation enough for you to try to one-up the naysayers.*

10. *You want to leave a legacy. You aspire to live a bigger life, to make an impact, to make your presence known. As they say, if you're not building your own dream, you're building someone else's.*

11. *You possess an incredible work ethic. If you don't mind putting in 12-hour days multiple times a week (as people do when starting a business), then why not put that to work for something you're really enthused about?*

12. *You want to control your time. Maybe you're most productive from 4 a.m. to 9 a.m., or perhaps you're a night owl. Maybe you want to be at your daughter's soccer*

practice at 3 p.m. or your son's acting classes at 4 p.m. Instead of being told when to work and when to take breaks or a vacation, you could finally determine your schedule.

13. *You need to inspire. You're the person people turn to when they need advice or a little pick-me-up. Owning a business gives you the chance to inspire the people who surround you.*

14. *You don't mind getting your hands dirty. You'll have to do plenty of grunt work as a new business owner. It's not always enjoyable, but you find it rewarding to see the fruits of your labor.*

15. *You enjoy problem solving. You are the first to jump in with fresh ideas when it comes to challenges.*

16. *You love to learn. You are always searching for the latest information on your industry. You would rather stay up late reading a trade journal or browsing educational videos than watching* Housewives of ________ *(fill in the blank).*

17. *You love* Shark Tank. *You make every one of your family members sit down with you as you dissect every concept and offer. You yell at the entrepreneurs when they take a bad deal or walk away from a good one. You say to yourself, "I could do better!"*

18. *You can multitask. This is part of the reason women make great entrepreneurs. If you're one of those who doesn't collapse under the pressure of multitasking, then you're already on your way.*

19. *You're not afraid of failure. You will fail daily as a business owner. Get used to it. It's the failures that teach you the most valuable lessons. You understand that failure is temporary. You are determined to make it happen and resilient when you get knocked down.*

20. *You work in a volatile industry. You're noticing that one of the worst things about working for someone else is contemplating the possibility of the company being bought, sold, or downsized, all of which may land you in the unemployment line. When I went through three layoffs by the age of 30, I realized that building my own business was no more risky than working for someone else.*

21. *You hate paying taxes. You realize you can write off a heck of a lot in your business. If you have a spouse that has a traditional J-O-B, your business losses can offset your tax obligations (as long as you're not a C corporation).*

22. *You're a born leader. Having a great idea is one thing. Being able to communicate that idea and convince others to jump on board is another. If you have the leadership skills to round up the troops and motivate them, consider starting your own venture.*

23. *You are exhilarated by achieving results. You're good at goal setting and driven to work towards achieving your goals. You get a charge when you accomplish what you set out to do, and you want more. But don't forget to let yourself celebrate and relish in the success!*

Chapter 5
Mindset

I'M EXCITED TO WORK with you on this extraordinary journey. While there are a million articles, books, and how-to guides on becoming more productive, fitter, happier, and so on, I believe that to be truly successful and live life to the fullest, it all starts with our mindset. The key to success is our ability to control our thoughts and master our psychology; everything else is a by-product of that process. If you can do that, you will open the doors to success, love, money, wealth, and everything you have ever been dreaming of.

First, all human beings have limiting beliefs—that is, false beliefs that are the result of their environment and that they hold as true. For instance, some people believe that money is evil and that rich people are all corrupt. Others believe that they are not smart enough, strong enough, confident enough, talented enough, or don't come from the right background. All those beliefs are difficult to change, first because we might not be aware of them and the profound impact they have on us, and second because they are located deep down in our subconscious, and thus cannot be accessed easily. However, learning how to overcome limiting beliefs is essential to becoming an entrepreneur.

There Is No Skill You Cannot Learn

People who can get rid of most of their limiting beliefs will gradually realize that the only obstacle that prevents them from being successful is themselves. In reality, we all have (more or less) the same brains. Thousands of people of average intelligence have accomplished great things throughout history.

I certainly put myself in the "average intellect" category. No, I'm not putting myself down; I truly have an average IQ and got (at best) average grades in school. What I know and appreciate is that this is in no way a determinant of my success. I have many other attributes: a tremendous amount of common sense, a fair amount of charisma, and a good dose of discipline, which all adds up to a high level of confidence. Yep, I said it—I'm very confident in myself. I have a confident mindset. Sure, there are plenty of things I don't know how to do, but I'm confident enough in my ability to "figure it out." I'm willing—or, perhaps as some would say, just dumb enough—to jump in and try!

For me, it's about "perspective." One of my favorite quotes is from Dr. Wayne W. Dyer: "Change the way you look at things and the things you look at change." This is a powerful statement. I learned this all too well after my car accident, and again after my miscarriage, layoffs, and divorce.

I believe that we have all amazing capabilities. Unfortunately, many people are unaware of how much they could accomplish, if only they were clear about what they really want in life and consistently develop plans of action to achieve their goals. Most people spend more time planning their next trip to Costco than planning their escape from corporate life.

We will discuss visioning and planning in detail toward the end of this section.

LEAN OUT MOMENT

Cyndee Edwards

I definitely felt like I had my life mapped out after college. I was going to take my fancy communications degree, move to Los Angeles, and become a news reporter. I completed multiple internships in college at various news stations. I was on my way!

What happened after that is quite a different story than what I'd imagined. In fact, it's kind of discouraging. I fought for four years to break into the industry, doing odd jobs on the side to get by. I just knew someone was going to discover me!

One of those odd jobs was as a part-time receptionist at a well-known day spa, Burke Williams, in Santa Monica, California. At the same time, I started dating a guy who ran his own salon. One day we were brainstorming on my next steps, and out of the blue he said, "Have you ever had a facial?" I hadn't, so he booked one for me. I remember stepping into a dimly lit room that smelled incredible. It was just me and this beautiful woman with an amazing touch. The entire experience blew me away. The next day I enrolled in aesthetics school.

After school, I went to work as an educator for one of the largest skin-care manufacturers in the world. It was the perfect role for me, as it combined my new love with all that I had learned from my communications degree—public speaking and presentation skills. I was on stage!

But after several years, my entrepreneurial genes kicked in (my dad was a private-practice dentist all my life), and I longed to have something of my own. I transitioned out of education to get more hands-on experience in running a spa. It took me just six months to build up the confidence to open my own aesthetics practice, The Skin Stop.

Six years later, I have two locations on the Central Coast of California and hundreds of clients. For me, building my own business has given me a way to express my creativity. It has allowed me to showcase my skills, not only in my business but also in the larger business community. I've been so inspired that I recently took on the role as president of my local Chamber of Commerce so I can support others in their business growth and success. I love it!

ABOUT

After graduating from Cal Poly San Luis Obispo in Speech Communications, Cyndee Edwards spent many years pursuing a career in television news, interning at KSBY and KTLA. She produced and created television programs, including a news magazine for the City of El Segundo. Her career took a drastic turn in 2000 when she discovered the world of skincare. As a licensed skincare therapist, Cyndee worked for several renowned skincare companies and currently runs her own skincare business, The Skin Stop, with offices in Morro Bay and San Luis Obispo.

www.TheSkinStop.com

Our first expert contributor, Linda O'Keefe, will take you into the world mindset. She has built her practice by helping people "shift" their perspectives and lives!

Linda O'Keefe, Making A Radical Shift

There's a very funny story my mother used to recount about me as a child. I say it was funny; she would say it was one of the biggest frustrations of her mothering "career." On grocery day, she had no option but to cart all four of her young daughters to the store, two of them clinging to her legs, one holding her hand like a "good girl," and me, running up and down the aisles asking strangers very pointed questions, like "Do you like your job?" "Do you love your children?" I was four.

There was something inside me so early on that just wanted to know how people ticked, both in their personal and professional lives. It was a built-in passion that extended so clearly into my adulthood that I made a career, much to my father's chagrin, out of assisting others in pursuing their passions.

My entire family was my first group of "naysayers" who, to this day, won't talk or ask about my profession. Not only was I choosing a vocation they couldn't comprehend, but I was also choosing to be a (gasp!) entrepreneur. I was *so* flying in the face of our families' long and honored tradition of working 30–35 years with a stable institution (preferably governmental) and retiring with a pension. But I had received two important gifts early in my life: the recognition of a built-in passion to be in the "people business" and so much disapproval that my "fighter" was determined to prove I could do it regardless. I won't say the second one was pleasant, but it was a motivator! That motivation propelled me through both my bachelor's and master's degrees in social work and opening my first business in 1987:

Options for Growth, a center for various forms of transformative work.

Then the passion took over, and I expanded my education to life and organizational coaching, energy work, and professional speaking and writing, all while also founding three more businesses: Core Creatives, LLC; Casa Creamos, LLC; and Inspiration Station, LLC. In 2014, I founded A Radical Shift, Inc., a transformative process that blends psychology, spirituality, and brain science to reunite participants with their essential selves while letting go of what is nonessential. The thread throughout all my work is a passion for understanding and empowering people, particularly women, to get clear on who they truly are and to help them uncover ways to express this.

One of the biggest challenges my clients have is gaining that clarity. If they hear my childhood story, they inevitably comment on how hard it seems to map back to who they truly are. And there's truth to that. The more we operate and function in the "grown-up," 3-D world of expectations, competition, responsibilities, obligations, etc., the less we remember the sparks we felt. But those sparks are there, and getting full clarity on what they are and how it feels to focus on them is the #1 key in beginning and maintaining forward movement.

Years ago, I coached a 41-year-old sales executive named Mary. She had started in sales right out of college and worked her way through the ranks to become a high-level executive in the company. Her salary and bonuses were more than ample, and she was respected in the workplace, but, she reported, getting motivated to go to work every day had become a chore. She didn't care about the product her company sold and daily would ask herself the question: "Is this all there is?" She had flirted with the idea of "going out on her own," but doing exactly what? When I asked her if she could identify anything in her work that she enjoyed, it just took a moment before a small grin formed. "I love coaching the sales team to dig deep and perform at their highest level. The best moment is I when I see that look on their faces, when they light up and 'get it.'" I asked her to stop for moment and really experience that feeling. As she did, I asked her to imagine what it would be like if she could experience that every day in her work. "It would be amazing!" And from there, (with help and support) she set up her own successful consulting business. Later, she let me know that every time she hit a roadblock, she would revisit that feeling and remember *why* she created her own business. It would help push her through almost anything.

Of course, how we handle roadblocks (on the inside or outside) is another key factor in moving forward:

1. **Recognize your mindset and shift it:** We have all experienced the process of goal setting (New Year's resolutions, anyone?) and attempting to stick with them. Our conscious mind is on board, but studies have shown that our subconscious mind dictates more than 90 percent of our life, and it fights hard to maintain current habitual thinking or action. One of the most powerful ways to get around this block is to use our imaginations. As an exercise, consider your job/corporate thinking and try to shift it to the mindset of an entrepreneur. For example:
    - From answering to your external boss TO following your internal leader
    - From earning money from hours worked TO creating financial compensation from your own efforts

- o From following the plan of your company TO creating a plan and work that you can love

Create a statement that affirms the mindset you are shifting *to*:

I trust and follow the leader in me to create a plan for work that I love and the generous financial compensation that flows from my efforts.

Combine the repetition of this statement with a one-minute visual of its reality. "See" yourself creating a business doing what you love, leading with confidence, and receiving money, feeling deeply the satisfaction that comes from all of those shifts.

2. Deal with the naysayers: The truth is that many people, even those closest to you, will not hesitate to tell you why you should not move forward with your new venture. It's important to prepare for that by recognizing that it's about their own fear(s), not about you. Be clear about your response.

I give my clients this exercise: Prepare a response that you can give as soon as you hear the fears, and use it like a mantra. For instance: "I hear that you are concerned. I've done my homework, have good guidance and am clear about my direction. Thanks anyway."

Remember: you become who you surround yourself with. This goes double when you are flying even a little outside of the everyday box. Your success as an entrepreneur can grow exponentially by being selective about who you interact with, understanding and using the power of networks, and actively pursuing the many avenues to connecting with others of "like mind."

Entrepreneurship is on the rise, and women are leading the pack. Finding and engaging with female entrepreneurs needs to be in the top five "to-dos" of preparation, ongoing support, and growth. Begin with any women already in your network or social circle who are successful entrepreneurs. Also, seek out Meetup groups, women-owned business groups within your local SBA, mastermind groups, etc. When you are actively looking for these resources and asking questions, it will be surprising how many you will find. I was lucky enough to "stumble" on to Hera Hub, where all of this, and more, is supported at the highest level.

Now is the time to get out a pen and paper. It is important to take the time to do this exercise and the others that will follow so you can craft your "flight path." It won't take long... I promise!

3-"D" Exercise - Dump, Discern & Detach

1. **Dump**

Set aside 30 minutes in a quiet, beautiful space where you will not be interrupted or distracted. Have a piece of paper and pen available. On the top of the paper, write, "When I consider starting my own business, I hear myself thinking ..."

Take a deep breath and write down every thought that comes into your mind after rereading that prompt. Keep writing until there are no more thoughts coming up.

Once you are finished, take another deep breath.

2. **Discern**

Next, you are going to review each item you wrote down, note your emotional reaction, and make two discernments:

Sort out the items that indicate a fear and rewrite them below your first list. Examples: I worry about financial security; I'm overwhelmed just imagining what I'll have to do; etc.

Take the fear list and, using a scale of 1–10, rank the initial level of discomfort you have right after reading the item. Remember that your body is a good indicator of reactions.

The highest-ranking fears are your block indicators. That awareness is really valuable. We cannot deal with what we don't fully know.

3. Detach

Look at your fears that showed up and take a couple of deep breaths. Allow your eyes to close and visualize those fears contained in a box. Then move away, in your mind's eye, from the box and look down on it from above. Hold that, and when you "come back," you can approach strategies/actions more neutrally.

ABOUT LINDA

Linda O'Keefe's experience in the personal and professional transformation field has spanned 27 years. With a Master's in Social Work and a certification in Ontological Coaching, she is committed to creating sustainable change and growth for individuals, couples and Organizational clients. Creator and Founder of numerous companies, she began Options For Growth in 1987, which still offers counseling, Coaching and cutting edge courses for those serious about discovering who they truly are. Her latest entrepreneurial endeavor is A Radical Shift, Inc., a transformative process that blends psychology, spirituality and brain science to remind participants of their essential self and to let go of anything they learned that gets in the way of them expressing that fully in the world. She believes passionately that alignment with the root of who we are, creates a life filled with meaning and grace on every level. Learn more at www.ARadicalShift.com.

LEAN OUT MOMENT

Dominique Molina, CPA, CTC

I remember it vividly, watching with intrigue as my mom wrote checks. I was so fascinated by how money worked that I started balancing my parent's checkbook at age eight.

When I went off to college, I needed a part-time job to support myself. I did everything from working in fast food to being a bank teller—all to the tune of $7 per hour. As I continued to learn about accounting while in school, I realized I could leverage what I was learning and make a heck of a lot more money, so I approached a couple of small businesses in my neighborhood and asked them if they needed bookkeeping help. I was able to land myself several part-time gigs and make three times as much money, which allowed me to work half the time and stay focused on my studies.

The only way I could earn my CPA license after graduating from college in 1999 was to go to work for an accounting firm. Despite my longing to continue to build my own business, I was essentially forced to go the corporate track.

To say it was male-dominated was an understatement. I learned quickly that if I wanted to move up the ladder, my car had better not leave the parking lot before 11:30 p.m. Knowing that I wanted to have a family someday, I knew the "partner track" was out of the question. The politics really kicked in when I didn't apply for several promotion opportunities. I didn't want to build someone else's business—I wanted to build my own. I quickly decided I would learn all I could and started planning my escape route.

Everyone I knew told me I was crazy when I quietly started to share my departure plans. Not even my parents or husband told me to "go for it," but I knew in my heart that I was designed to be an entrepreneur. I finally made the leap four years later when I had my son, Andrew.

I started my own CPA firm at age 27 and sold it six years later. Although my goal was to be a millionaire by age 30, it didn't come until long after. Since then, I've started several companies and supported hundreds of other entrepreneurs in building their dreams. Yes, it's taken a lot of hard work and many nights working past 11:30 p.m., but I wouldn't trade the opportunity for anything in the world!

ABOUT

Dominique Molina is the cofounder and president of the American Institute of Certified Tax Coaches. As the driving force and visionary behind the San Diego-based company, Ms. Molina set out to change the way tax professionals approach tax planning. In 2009, Ms. Molina began to create an elite network of tax professionals, including CPAs, EAs, attorneys, and financial service providers who are trained to help their clients proactively plan and implement tax strategies that can rescue thousands of dollars in wasted taxes. More than 12 years of hands-on experience in the accounting and business fields provide her with ample skills to accomplish this mission. Ms. Molina has successfully licensed tax professionals as Certified Tax Coaches across the country, creating a national network of highly qualified professionals who provide proactive service for their clients. This premier group of professionals features fewer than 400 specialists in 48 states who have achieved this very specialized designation.

www.CertifiedTaxCoach.com

Chapter 6
Fear

NOW THAT YOU'VE HAD a chance to work through Linda's exercise, and before we dive into the next key area of entrepreneurship, fighting fear, I want to introduce a new question:

Why don't you put yourself first?

Both boys and girls are taught from an early age to "share," but girls especially are taught to "be polite," "put others first," and to "not be selfish." Many of us also saw our mothers putting others first and essentially "doing it all." To avoid being judged as someone who "can't do it all," we do it all, trying to prove that we aren't selfish. We tell ourselves, "I have to make sure the dog is walked, my elderly neighbor is fine, and the dishes are washed and put away before I can sit down. I can't take a nap because I have to fold the laundry, pay the bills, and then run six miles to keep myself in shape. If I spend too much time working on the kids' homework with them (after chauffeuring them around all afternoon) and don't have a three-course meal ready and a perfectly clean house, what would my mother-in-law think?"

In many ways, we feel good about all of the sacrifices we're making in the name of serving everyone else, and our guilt about having our own needs and desires is made less intense for a moment. Even worse, some of us don't have the self-love to believe we are important enough to let others know about "our needs", so we continue to put ourselves last. This is *not* the "servant leadership" I was talking about in the prior section.

When you put yourself last, you have nothing left to offer. Before you take out your organizer or make another to-do list, realize that you don't need more "balance" to be happy. You need a breakthrough—you need a *reinvention*! What I'm talking about is a shift in thinking, a change in mindset that says it's OK to love yourself, ask for help, say no, and not be perfect!

Leading By Example

Do you have children? If so, my question for you is, what are you modeling for your children? If you put yourself last, what are you teaching them? In reality, you are teaching girls that they should do the same, and you are teaching boys that they should eventually find a partner that acts like you.

Furthermore, what kind of example are you setting if you tell them anything is possible, but don't *show* them anything is possible? Don't fall into the trap of "anything is possible, except for me."

Face Your Fears And Do It Anyway

I can hear you saying, "But I have a mortgage and kids to feed!" They will live—I promise!

When I set off to be a "free agent", I was the sole breadwinner of my family. In fact, as I mentioned previously, my husband was a negative contributor to our income—meaning he spent more every month than he made. I finally realized, at age 30, that putting myself last was not the way to get ahead.

Yes, I initially had to learn to live with less—no more going out to lunch and getting my nails done weekly. It was time to buckle down for the sake of having control of my own destiny. Although it wasn't easy, it was well worth it. I cobbled it together by picking up a couple other part-time teaching jobs and hustled to build my network. I was *free*!

Many people become so embedded in the rat race that they can't dig themselves out—they become corporate slaves. Their focus is on the exterior and what other people think of them, driving them to buy fancy cars and big houses, with the belief that these "things" will make them happy. It never does.

Depending the on type of venture, you don't need to have tens of thousands of dollars to start a business. However, you can't start a business until you break your fancy spending habits. I want you to take your focus off the exterior and shine the light on *you*—not you in your Trina Turk dress—just *you*.

Sorry to be so blunt, but it breaks my heart to meet people with a ton of passion about dozens of ideas and they are afraid to leave their safe, secure J-O-B. We have helped many of these women at Hera Hub by supporting them with education, resources, and connections as they side-launch their businesses. Sadly, many of these women don't stay focused and they never take the leap—because they are afraid of the unknown.

I feel fortunate—getting laid off three times in my 20s taught me that the risky path is putting all your eggs in one basket with an employer, leaving your destiny up to someone else's decisions.

So I ask you: How will you put yourself first?

LEAN OUT MOMENT

Violet Rainwater

I'm in love with sales! I love teaching, sharing, and educating anyone who will listen. I've been a top producer in every job I've had for the last 15 years, and while I've always had a J-O-B, I've also always wanted to launch my own business. In fact, I've been trying to side-launch a business for the last ten years!

The decision to take the leap was put on hold because I was the mother of three children and the primary breadwinner for the family. I just couldn't take the leap, but I did decide to start building—slowly, on the side. I started by blogging and making videos about my passion. I started sharing what I had learned during this very lucrative career. My mindset was different than anyone else's in the business: I used yoga and breath work to put me in a space that ultimately allowed me to approach the market from an entirely different angle. I want to share this with the world!

The sales profession is "hero to zero" every single month. Yes, sales can be cutthroat, but in the past, being a top producer in your firm meant job security. Not any more! My final "lean-out" moment was when I was let go from a sales job where I was a top producer in the company—number one on the West Coast. The world of financial services has changed dramatically since 2008, and with the loads of compliance hoops one must jump through, it was almost impossible to get every "i" dotted and every "t" crossed. Ultimately, they let me go on a compliance technicality to cover their behinds. As always, it stung at first, but it was the best thing that ever happened to me.

That situation finally woke me up to the fact that I could do it on my own! It was my time to build my legacy versus carrying out someone else's vision. So, at age 41, I finally launched Rainmaker Way, a sales training company that specializes in training financial services professionals to master the art of sales.

ABOUT

Violet Rainwater is the Founder and Chief Rainmaker of Rainmaker Way. Leveraging more than 25 years as an award-winning sales professional, Violet assists financial professionals with driving sales by driving tremendous value. Using her financial expertise and passion for innovative sales strategies, Violet Rainwater is Making it Rain by changing the game.

www.TheRainmakerWay.com

Deirdre Maloney - Fighting and Overcoming Fear

I was born into a fear-filled house. Yep, we were "fear-*full*". The reason was that my parents (and in particular, my lovely, nervous, Italian, New York-based mother) didn't want anything bad to happen to me. As she'll say to this day, all of that fear has been there because she loves me so much, sees herself as my protector. And so the best strategy she could find to keep bad things from happening to me was to keep me from doing anything that could go badly. Which meant avoiding anything new, uncertain, or risky.

And her definition of risky? Let's just say it was (and is, to this day) anything that might, perhaps, lead to physical or mental pain or anguish of any kind at some point sometime soon or later on!

I submit to you an example. When I was about five years old and living on Long Island, I was simply walking down the street to my friend Leslie's house. It was about five houses down from where we lived. My mother walked me to the end of our driveway, then watched me walk down the street. When I got to Leslie's house, I turned around, waved good-bye, then walked up the driveway, where I was hidden by trees so Mom couldn't see me. Then I did what I had been instructed to do—I called her immediately when I got inside so that she'd know I hadn't been kidnapped.

Seriously.

Again, I want to say that the fear that surrounded the Maloney house was put there out of love. I also know that our definition of *risk* wasn't unique. In fact, many who live in New York with a somewhat nervous Italian-or-other-similarly-cultured mother can undoubtedly relate. The problem was that the often-paralyzing fear that accompanied anything new or uncertain led me to choose *not* to do anything new or uncertain. Even worse, the words "you shouldn't do" something because of the risk soon became translated to me as "you can't do" something because you're not capable of handling the potential consequences.

I lived with this belief for decades. The saddest part about all of this is I've always had an ingrained desire to explore new places, meet new people, and engage in new experiences. None of which I did for a long time.

Eventually, however, I got over it.

The transition from fearful to fearless took time. It first began when I went away to college, and then began in earnest when I permanently moved away from home after the ending of my (brief) first marriage.

It wasn't an easy decision to leave New York. My family is a loving and supportive one, and leaving them was both sad and scary. But when my second husband (herein referred to as "Hubby") and I got together, we knew it would make sense to start our partnership in a new place. We chose Colorado—a state located far, far away from New York.

What happened next was I began to slowly do what I'd always wanted to do—to reach outside of my comfort zone, to explore new places, meet new people, and engage in new experiences. I often did these things with Hubby. Sometimes I did them alone. In the early years of my "fear transition," each step felt fraught, terrifying, and exhilarating. Taking a new job that stretched me, traveling to a foreign country, writing my first book, and eventually starting my own business—each of these felt dangerous. Each felt uncomfortable. Each felt risky, like I could get hurt, feel disappointed, embarrass myself. With each of these new steps, I moved further on the journey to fear*less*. And that's because I learned some critical things about fear.

1. Fear is about the future

When it comes down to it, we don't fear things that are happening to us right now. Right now, we are dealing with whatever we need to deal with *right now*. When we fear a consequence, when we worry that starting our own business will land us on the streets, when we believe that submitting a book idea will lead to rejection, when we entertain the idea that attending a new networking group will lead us to isolation and embarrassment all night, we are imagining something going badly sometime in the future. The truth is that, right now, we are fine. We are dealing with life. We are doing what we have to do. The future is in our imagination. And boy, can our imaginations muster up some colorful consequences! When we make thoughtful decisions, weigh our pros and cons, and make clear, strong choices about the future, then the fears we have about what *might happen* don't matter. We will deal with them if we need to. Which leads me to my next point …

2. Bad things do happen

I have to give this one to Mom. She was right. Bad things do happen sometimes. Ironically, I've found this realization to be quite liberating. After all, the fact that bad things do happen takes away the need to control every single thing in life to keep the bad stuff away. It's just impossible. For some reason, many of us believe that all of that bad stuff that happened in the past is the end of the bad stuff, and nothing bad will ever happen again if we just keep our heads in the game. Nope. Bad stuff will happen. Things won't go your way, and this is true for the business that you'll create. Sometimes you'll get rejected, and sometimes you'll mess up a project, and sometimes you'll be embarrassed. Sometimes you'll make people mad. It's all part of life, and it's unavoidable. So know that. Do your best to make careful decisions, but then go with those decisions.

And know that, no matter what the bad thing is and when it happens, you can handle it. When things go badly, you find out just how strong you are. Really, you have no other choice. When your business has a bad month, you strategize new marketing ideas. When you get rejected, you move on to a new opportunity. Nobody has the luxury or the desire to sit paralyzed on the couch for the rest of one's life when a bad thing happens. You have no choice but to move on. And you will. And when you do, I promise, the bad stuff won't feel nearly as bad once it's in your memory banks. Time has a way of putting these things in perspective.

By the way, if you don't believe you can handle the bad stuff, then avoiding risk isn't the answer. The answer is learning for real that you *can* handle it. You must take steps and engage in resources to help you recognize and embrace how amazing and capable you are. You must know that entrepreneurship is just one more thing to learn about, one more thing that will stretch and grow you, one more thing that you are completely capable of handling. And if it doesn't go well, then you can handle that, too. You must know this, and you must surround yourself with others who know this, too, so they can remind you when you forget it.

You must do these things. They are two critical keys to a happy life.

3. Bad things aren't bad

The truth is that the bad stuff is the rich stuff. It's the juicy stuff. It's the awesome-dinner-party-story stuff.

In 2014 I spent six months overseas, and while I was away, I wound up in an emergency room in a small town in France. I don't speak French, and they didn't speak English, but we worked it out. Even though it wasn't fun at the moment, of all the stories from those six months, that's the one I tell the most. Because we all figured out how to communicate. And I got better. And once again I learned that I can handle things. And, well, it's a pretty funny story when you hear it from start to finish.

As "bad" as it feels in the moment, the "bad stuff" is the stuff that helps us learn. It helps us experience. It helps us grow. It's the stuff we remember. It's the stuff that makes us who we are. It's the stuff that makes us know what we can handle.

And it's the stuff that makes the good stuff that much sweeter. Just ask Hubby. There isn't a day that goes by when he doesn't benefit from the fact that my first marriage was so challenging. Relatively speaking, I know every day that I'm lucky to be where I am now, with him.

When bad stuff happens with your business, you'll wince for a day—then you'll learn from it and make your business even better. The bad stuff won't just fade away, but it will provide the seeds and soil to help you grow in ways you never could've before.

Like it or not.

Exercise: Let's Bust Your Fear

It's time to transition from fearful to fearless. You must experience life knowing that life is meant to be *experienced*. For real. There's so much rich stuff out there waiting for you—businesses to build, people to meet, projects to create.

Let's get you started, yes?

This exercise is designed to help you recognize the lessons you learned about fear and risk throughout your life, and to help you bust through the ones that are holding you back. (Note: I use the word *parents* in the exercise, but depending on your situation, feel free to replace it with whoever was your primary guardian growing up.)

1. What is your earliest memory of getting hurt as a child? How did your parents respond to the situation? How did this impact your beliefs about risk?

2. Think back to a time during your early childhood years when you wanted to try something new. How did your parents respond? How did this impact your beliefs about yourself and your ability to handle situations?

3. Think back to a time when you were a teenager and wanted to try or join something new. How did you feel about the opportunity? How did your parents respond? How did your friends respond? How did this impact your beliefs about yourself and your ability to handle situations?

4. Write a list of the top three fears that have been on your mind over the past month. Are they about things that might happen in the future? How might you handle them if they do happen?

5. How are you doing right now? What are you dealing with in this moment? What does this tell you about your ability to handle things in the present?

6. Write a list of the top three worst things that have happened to you in the past. What have you learned from them? What have you learned about yourself by going through them? How are you different today as a result? As painful as they were, how is your life better because they happened?

7. Are there any beliefs about risk that you feel you need to let go of? What are they?

8. Write the beliefs from above on a piece of paper, then burn or rip up the paper. Do it with a supportive friend. Wave good-bye. Then find the perfect books, podcasts, presentations, or affirmations to help you build that self-esteem and embrace how awesome you are. And congratulate yourself for doing so. Life is about to get better as a result.

ABOUT DEIRDRE

Deirdre Maloney is a bliss builder, using her personal brand of "mild audacity" to help people find their truth and live a happier, more successful life. She does it through her work as a published author, national speaker, and proud president of her training and facilitation company, Momentum LLC. Deirdre's popular blog on all things leadership, a regular feature on huffingtonpost.com, is a hit with anyone who likes a direct, authentic style with their morning coffee. She has published several books, including Bogus Balance: Your Journey to Real Work/Life Bliss. *For more on Deirdre, visit www.MakeMomentum.com.*

LEAN OUT MOMENT

Carmen Chavez de Hesse

It was 6 a.m. on a weekday, and I was meeting with a locksmith to change the locks on a franchise that had defaulted. This task fell to me as the operations director of a franchise holding company. The franchise had been providing daycare and boarding services for dogs. I'm an animal lover, which made this task all the more difficult, but beneath the difficulty was a determination to turn this business around. Over a challenging six-month period, I led the rebuilding of the franchise and worked closely with its team members to increase revenues by 40 percent. It was immensely gratifying to see the fruits of my labor and watch a business come full circle.

One day, I was watching 20 dogs at play when it hit me: I've got this! I realized that my 12 years as an operations director had been, in actuality, an apprenticeship. I'd worked in all phases of franchising, and I had good relationships with many people in the franchising world. The adventure of rebuilding a franchise was proof that I had the skills needed to run my own business. This was the first time I seriously considered becoming an entrepreneur.

As part of my "apprenticeship," I carried an intense workload for less pay to justify a rather flexible schedule. The flexibility enabled me to pursue IVF (in vitro fertilization) treatments, which required time off from work. After my daughter was born, I knew that returning to my demanding job would mean sacrificing my priorities of health and family. Becoming an entrepreneur would let my priorities remain priorities.

While still working as an operations director, I began networking with several small businesses that were interested in franchising. When two of them signed contracts with me, I knew it was time to make the leap to full-time entrepreneur. I set up my franchise consulting business and found Hera Hub, where I could network and collaborate with other women entrepreneurs. Advice and mentoring came from industry peers and family members. In fact, my number-one mentor is my father-in-law, who retired from IBM-Peru and is now a business consultant.

Being an entrepreneur means seeing my dreams in action and staying in sync with my top priorities. As a business owner, I work as an expert, not an apprentice. I get to pursue my passion for helping others realize their dreams of franchising their business, and I have the flexibility to enjoy my number-one passion—raising my beautiful daughter Marina.

ABOUT

Carmen Chavez de Hesse brings more than 20 years of experience in business development, franchising, and coaching to her work with multi-unit brands in a variety of industries, including food, real estate, animal services, and health and wellness. She has helped to grow several national brands and works as a legal liaison to assist master franchisors with FDD filing, brand compliance, and contract execution/dissolution.

www.linkedin.com/in/carmenchavezdehesse

Before we move on, I want to introduce one more thought related to fear: say "yes", and figure it out—otherwise known as...

Fake It 'til You Make It

I can say from personal experience that I believe wholeheartedly in this concept—it's how I discovered my passion!

One of these experiences came through a little white lie. It was early 2005 when I attended a business breakfast meeting and met Linda Lattimore, a local attorney. After the event, as we were talking about business, she leaned over and asked me, "Do you golf?" I sat up a little straighter and said, "Yes, I'm learning," which actually wasn't true. I had been thinking about starting to golf, as the man I was dating at the time golfed and I thought it would make sense to acquire the skill—as if it's something one just picks up in a weekend! She invited me to join her and a group of women the following weekend. She assured me there were many beginners in the group and we were playing a scramble—meaning it was a group effort to get the little white ball in the hole. This wasn't too daunting and sounded like a good way to start.

My boyfriend was elated that I wanted to learn how to golf. He quickly outfitted me with clubs and decked me out in the appropriate attire. I had no idea what I was doing, but I looked the part!

I showed up at the Lomas Santa Fe Executive golf course at 7 am and found myself meeting the most amazing group of women. There were dozens of other "free agents" and entrepreneurs, many of whom were meeting for the first time. We went out and played nine holes of golf (my first time on the course) and had a blast!

I'm sure glad I faked it, because this experience gave me the courage to to "begin."

Yes, Others Have Faked It...

Estee Lauder is a classic example of "fake it 'til you make it." For years, she told the media that she was a countess of genteel

European background. Lauder finally "came clean" in her autobiography, *Estee: A Success Story.*

In truth, Josephine Esther Mentzer was born in 1908 in Queens, New York. While her parents, Max Mentzer and Rose (Schotz) Mentzer, were Jewish immigrants from Hungary and Czechoslovakia, they were far from high society. Her father owned a hardware store, above which the family lived.

Estee Lauder was famous for such statements as, "Don't be afraid of the trial-and-error approach," which she claimed was a big part of her success. But the real reason Lauder succeeded where others failed is that she simply refused to give up. When she wanted something, she was known to resort to some highly creative tactics to get it. She used one such tactic to break the prestigious Galleries Lafayette account in Paris. When the manager refused to stock her products, Lauder 'accidentally' spilled her Youth Dew fragrance on the floor during a demonstration in the middle of a crowd. As the appealing scent wafted through the air, it quickly aroused the interest of customers, who began asking where they could purchase the product. Seeing this, the manager agreed to give Lauder an initial order.

By the mid-1950s, Youth Dew accounted for 80 percent of Estee Lauder's sales and had transformed the fledgling company into a multimillion-dollar business. The fake-it-'til-you-make-it approach made Lauder the wealthiest self-made woman in America and created a family dynasty that continues today.

Still Not Feeling It? Then Try The Power Pose …

If you haven't seen the TED talk by Amy Cuddy, I highly recommend it. Search for "Your body language shapes who you are." Cuddy shows how simply stepping into an opportunity and doing what she calls a "power pose" makes you feel more confident. I suggest you try it, right now!

Chapter 7
Passion

IT TOOK ME 35 years and a lot of bumps in the road to recognize my passion. I say "recognize" because I don't think we find our passion, but rather go through a series of experiences that help us draw it out. A colleague of mine used to say, "You don't find your passion you take it with you in everything you do." That still resonates with me to this day.

Ironically, one of my most memorable "fake-it-'til-you-make-it" moments also helped me uncover my passion. That little white lie that I could golf turned into a huge opportunity for me to recognize my passion for collecting, connecting, and leading. Linda Lattimore was an important role model and mentor to me at a critical time in my life. I'm forever grateful.

Your Turn…

Finding, igniting, discovering, or revealing your passion (whatever your approach!) is a critical part of launching your business. This is why two "passion experts" will be providing different, and yet equally valuable, perspectives in the following section. The first is presented by Sara Clark-Williams and the second is by Debby Eubank. I'm certain you will find these very personal and powerful viewpoints helpful as you hone in on your own unique passion.

Sara Clark-Williams - Finding Your Sweet Spot

From a young age, I knew I had a calling to help people. I have a deep, faith-based belief that each and every human being is loved, precious, and has unique qualities and gifts to offer the world—that every person has a purpose! This deep belief only grew as I got older. I see value and potential when I look at each person I interact with. The opportunity to help others recognize their value, potential, purpose, and passion is so fulfilling for me.

As a teenager, I noticed my struggles with procrastination and focusing on tasks. I began to explore how to overcome procrastination and soon began writing my own goals for the year, and I haven't stopped since (I was 16 years old). At the same time, being a girl in leadership positions (both in my church community and academically), I started noticing gender and personality differences. I soaked up the books I read on personality and communication in relationships. That's when I knew I wanted to major in psychology.

My first professional job was with a reputable non profit organization, teaching women in recovery how to rebuild their lives. This ranged from communication skills, to goal setting, to career exploration. I facilitated three-hour workshops on these topics at other social service organizations within the community. At first, I was terrified—but I did it anyway. The experience of pushing through the fear to get a meaningful message across was a pivotal part of my personal growth. I was stretched, and I was so grateful for the experience.

After two years of doing this, I knew I needed to fulfill my potential in a greater way. I considered going back to school to become a therapist; however, after working with clients in need and having coworkers who were case managers, social workers, and therapists, I took a hard look at myself and whether I was a fit with the day-to-day reality of that work.

I discovered that the field of industrial-organizational psychology would allow me to help people from a different angle, so I took two years to go back to school and get my master's degree. I had the experience within my program of working several internships—all within organizations of different industries and sizes. Since then, I've worked with hundreds of organizations, entrepreneurs, and individuals to clarify what they want, simplify the process of achieving that, and support them to grow their capacity to become greater.

I love people, and I feel called to instill in others that they are loved, capable, and free to choose a life they love. I believe that with choice comes both freedom and responsibility. My life purpose, conveyed in a one-liner, is "to encourage, inspire, and equip people to fulfill their potential." Part of that process is recognizing their potential—what's possible, their capacity for becoming their greatest selves.

A core part of becoming greater is understanding yourself—not only your gifts and talents, but also what you're passionate about. A key part of the work I do with my coaching clients is discovering the overlapping area where skills, interests, and passions intersect. That's where the powerful stuff is. That's where you can find what lights you up to the greatest level and therefore where you can make your greatest impact.

Sadly, many women don't have this knowledge about themselves and continue to live a life that's "good enough", always feeling that something is missing. Others may find out this information but don't know what to do with it. In either case, it pains me to imagine this. This is why I support women in discovering who they are and what they are passionate about—so they can live full lives, not only for themselves, but also for the impact they can then have on others in a positive way. Wherever you are in your life or entrepreneurial journey, such clarity frees you up to bring more of that into your life—whether through volunteering, a fun self-expression project outside of your "day job," or in your unique approach with your clients.

It's when women "see" this overlapping area that they understand what their deepest passions are and what their deepest calling is. This is often when women see what they are meant to do as a business, or, for current entrepreneurs, where they can focus more in their business to feel more fulfilled and make a bigger impact. There's nothing like seeing someone light up when they "see" and acknowledge what they are truly passionate about for the first time, in a new way, or even *how* they can bring more of that into their life and business. The female entrepreneurs I work with often are passionate about the work they're doing but tend to separate the passion for their exact work from other things they personally feel passionate about. I encourage my clients and others to find creative ways to bring more of who they are into their work and business overall. It is often what makes one business stand out from another in the same industry, and makes business even more fulfilling!

Explore, cultivate, and ignite your passion *on purpose*!

The biggest factor for me in recognizing my own passion was being in tune with myself and my experiences and living life very proactively. In other words, some people just float through life; that's not me. I can look back and see common threads at various points in my life and entrepreneurial journey—the consistent things, the stepping stones that led me to this point. When I can see those common threads, it's amazing how things have synergized along the way. Nothing is a waste of time unless you do nothing with it.

The process of discovering your passions is a lifelong journey—as you push out of your comfort zones and explore and try new things, you are naturally going to discover new passions. It's ongoing!

Sometimes you recognize your passions when you're doing something that you're obviously not passionate about, or in a situation that seems to suck the passion right out of you. That was the case for me professionally after I had accepted a great job just after completing graduate school.

After a couple of years at my job, I realized that a corporate environment wasn't for me. I needed to be part of something meaningful to me personally and do work that was both head- and heart-based. My corporate job didn't allow for much heart. It began to suck the life out of me, and I *knew* I was meant for more! It was the pain of feeling squashed and that my passion was being suppressed in that environment. Ultimately, I knew I wasn't shining my brightest, and I couldn't continue along that path with this knowledge.

I began working on developing my business on lunch hours and weekends. Then in August 2008, I took the leap! It was scary but *so* exciting. I am forever grateful for the courage to make that choice. It's times like these when I look back at my experiences, skills, and education and could see them synergizing! It's safe to say that most people want to be happy while making a difference, and I love that you don't have to choose between the two. I did it, and so can you!

Take some purposeful action now by completing the

Ignite Your Passion exercise. (I asked myself some of these questions during my entrepreneurial exploration while at my corporate job).

Questions to Ignite Your Passion!

As adults, it's easy to downplay things we're passionate about because they don't make money, they're silly, we don't have time for them, etc. I invite you to open your mind to freely respond to the questions that follow, and don't hold back. No filtering to sound good. Give yourself the freedom to respond with total honesty and transparency.

1. If you truly felt "alive," what would be true? Why?
2. If you were living your life to the fullest, what would be true? Why?
3. What is one thing you can do to start living your life to the fullest?
4. If you could do anything you wanted to do and money didn't matter, what would you do?
5. Recall the last time you got "lost" in what you were doing.
6. What message is bubbling up inside of you that you feel compelled to share with the world?
7. Take a look back at all the things you wrote for the previous questions. Then respond (write, draw, doodle!) confidently to the sentence below:
   I am passionate about:

Woohoo! You did it. How did that feel? Any new insights? Consider posting your responses to the last question where you can see them easily and quickly to keep yourself aware of bringing more of those core things you love into your life and work. If this resonated with you, I'd love to hear from you. Feel free to contact me at sara@fabfempreneurs.com.

Whether you're currently an entrepreneur or just starting to work on creating your business idea, there are four things you need to develop and stay in touch with to truly have a balanced, fulfilling business that also makes money: Head, Heart, Habits, and Hub. You can see all four and how they overlap in my Fab 4 Framework that follows. Heart is where the passion comes in, and it's one of the four things you must bring to your entrepreneurial journey every day. The fact is, when it's missing, you're not bringing your best and won't have the greatest impact nor the greatest results you desire (in other words, you won't be in your "sweet spot"). To learn more about the Fab 4 Framework and how you can be in your sweet spot, go to www.FabFempreneurs.com and take my free business self-assessment, designed for entrepreneurs at every stage.

ABOUT SARA

In 2012 Sara founded her second business, Fab Fempreneurs, where she supports female entrepreneurs to find the "sweet spot" in their business. With a BA in Psychology and a Master's in Industrial-Organizational Psychology, she has coached and consulted with hundreds of individuals, organizations, and entrepreneurs to achieve greater levels of success in their personal and professional lives. Whether you're a newer entrepreneur and looking to get momentum going and your business growing or an established entrepreneur and want to see more of your big vision come to fruition, Sara supports and guides you to make it happen! Learn more at www.FabFempreneurs.com

The Fab 4 Formula

Business success can seem like a secret recipe or an elusive aim. Whether your goals are humble or huge, whether you produce a product or service, whether you are a solopreneur or a leader of many, there are four domains that you must engage, align and implement in order to create a solid foundation for success and feel focused, fulfilled and financially successful. The Fab 4 Formula consists of: Head, Heart, Habits and Hub.

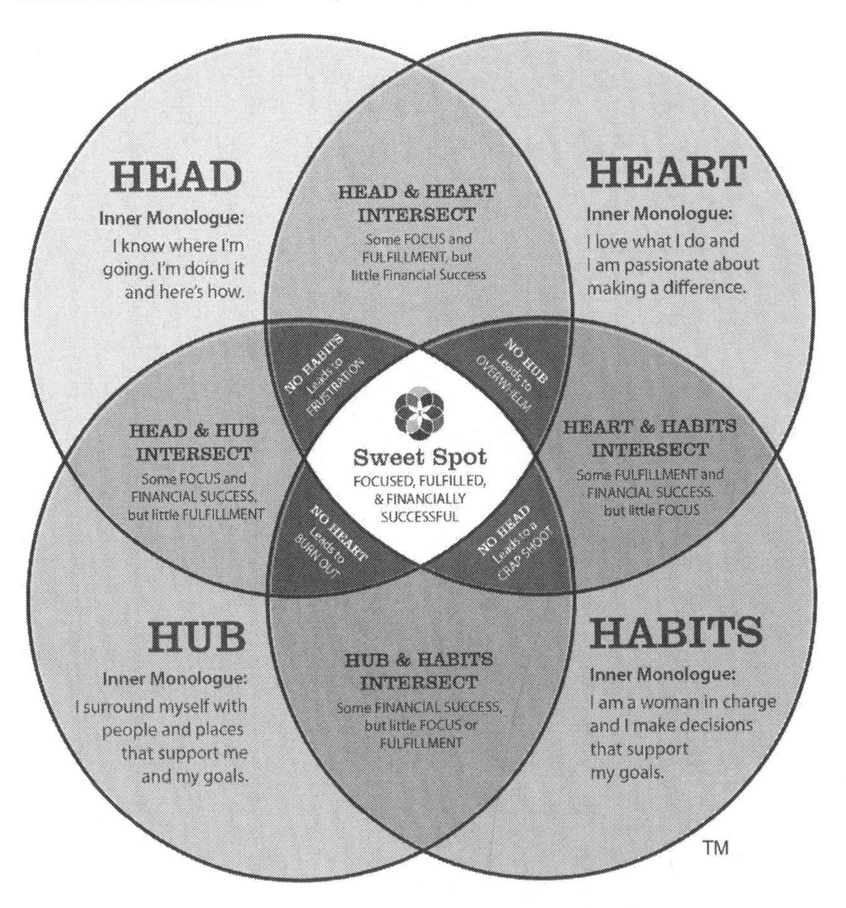

LEAN OUT MOMENT

Shelley Murasko

I followed all the Midwest advice given to me as a child—go to a good college, get on a solid career track at a big company, get married, and have children. All was going great with that plan, except I was not fulfilled in my work doing industrial operations for a large biotechnology company. I had risen within the company quickly, ultimately taking on a position as the Director of Global Operations.

While having my first child in 2008 (and my second 18 months after) was a factor in not taking a VP position that would require a significant amount of travel, I found it was more a lack of fulfillment that drove me. I remember dreading going back to work after my maternity leave, mostly because I just wasn't being challenged anymore. After being back just a few weeks, I was so tired of the corporate bureaucracy that I found myself just not showing up for important meetings.

Within two weeks of my return, I was desperate to try to figure out what was wrong with me, so I sought career counseling—ironically, through our Employee Assistance Program. Through the course of six meetings, it was clear that something had to shift in my work.

I had always been interested in investing. I bought every book I could get my hands on and read voraciously in my spare time. At one point, I tried to move into an investor relations role within my company, thinking that would pull the puzzle pieces together. When I didn't get that job, I realized I needed to create my own.

It took me a total of six years to move forward. The first task was getting my conservative husband on board. I knew

I needed to save money. Most people will tell you to save six months of living expenses—I saved three years. After a year of discussions, my husband asked, "Why don't you start a women's investment club and just get this out of your system?" I did that, and it still didn't quench my thirst. I then began seeking advice from those in financial services and continued to study everything I could in my spare time.

Finally, at age 42, I took the leap out of my stable corporate job to venture into the unknown. It certainly wasn't easy at first, but it has been one of the most rewarding things I've ever done. I'm now a certified financial advisor, working with great women, and building a business I love!

ABOUT

For two decades, Shelley served as a leader in the corporate realm of industrial engineering, using her talent for improving costs and driving revenues to deliver productivity to the bottom line of Fortune 500 companies. Always a passionate student of investing and personal finance, Shelley now directs her experience in planning, management, and analysis toward helping individual clients grow their wealth and move toward their financial goals. In 2013, Shelley completed her Financial Planning certificate from Bryant University. She bid farewell to her successful corporate career and accepted a Wealth Manager position at Bahr Investment Group, knowing she had come home to her true calling.

www.linkedin.com/in/bahrgroup

Now get ready for a slightly different approach to "revealing" your passion. What I like about Debby's story is the focus on finding your "niche."

Debby Eubank - The Big Reveal

Do you yearn to free yourself from a J-O-B, to fulfill a deeper passion and make a bigger impact in the world? After years of success in your corporate job and caring for others, is there now a part of you that is saying passionately, "It's my turn?"

Thinking of being in your shoes again and considering what would best support you, I realized I would have been so grateful to be told the shortcut to a successful passion-based business that I have learned and honed over the years. It might have helped me avoid the struggle, frustration, and pain that so many flailing passion-driven entrepreneurs experience. It must be said, however, that I don't personally regret for a moment any of my struggles or experiences, because they have led me right to here and now—to passionately living my life's purpose and making a difference in many women's lives.

Experience That Led To My Purpose and Work

This is what I've learned about passion-based business and success from first-hand experience in my own businesses, as well as the many private and group clients I've worked with over the years at Niche On Purpose.

Here's the shortcut! But first, let's define shortcut. It doesn't mean you won't work hard or that it won't take time to establish your business. The shortcut is that you won't spend a decade struggling to have a passion-based business that supports you! Instead, you can build from a solid foundation—your passion and value—and ultimately feel confident from the very beginning.

If your passion is connected to a specific problem and transformation, it has an inherently high value that people like yourself greatly desire and will invest in. My experience has been that if you attempt to turn your passion into a business and others do not see the clear value, it will be difficult to create a successful business around it.

You can have a passion without purpose, but you cannot have a purpose without passion.

Before I go further, I have to offer a word of caution: be wary of the saying, *"Do what you love and the money will come."* In my experience, this is an incomplete sentence. *"Build it and they will come"* is a myth, too. I know firsthand, and it was a painful experience—one I hope to help other women avoid by having their foundation solidly in place first.

This is what I know: if you can't articulate what you do, the value you offer, and whom you serve, your business cannot succeed. Unfortunately, after more than 15 years as an entrepreneur, I've come to know that not being able to articulate the value you offer (your big why/passion) to the people you serve and the specific problem you can solve (the outcome you specifically can provide) is perhaps the biggest problem entrepreneurs have.

To let this really land for you, I will share my personal experience with *not* having a business and offers that were truly in alignment with my purpose and passion. This resulted in years and years of financial struggle, stress-related health conditions, and, truthfully, what I call a "bankrupt" life. While there are other underlying issues related to self-worth and value that played an instrumental part in my struggles, as we are speaking about revealing your passion here, I will leave that for another day. I invite you to visit my website to learn more.

An exercise to begin revealing your passion (and possibly life's purpose) is provided for you after my story. This process will include looking at the areas of your life where you have had struggles and challenges ("breakdowns") and how you've overcome, transformed, and triumphed over them ("breakthroughs"). Pay attention in my personal story to my breakdowns and breakthroughs, as this will help give you an example of how to complete the exercise. It will also provide an understanding of the necessary steps to creating a successful business that you love and that supports you!

My Story: How I Revealed My Passion and Went From Struggling to Success

Having worked in corporate for 12 years, climbing the ladder and holding senior management positions at well-known financial institutions such as Bank of America, I was used to having high levels of responsibility. As an auditor and later a compliance manager, the responsibility landed on my shoulders (as the liaison between all state and federal regulatory agencies) to ensure we remained in compliance with all regulations and compliance-related operational procedures. Collaborating with senior management, all department heads, and the regulators— satisfying the regulations and rectifying infractions—was a comprehensive process.

I thrived and loved the challenge. I was driven and achieved my goal of a promotion every one or two years. I bought my first home at 30 years old in sunny San Diego. I drove luxury cars and by all accounts, I looked successful. However, eventually, living a life where I defined my self-worth by my job title— with a constant striving for achievement as well as workaholic and perfectionist tendencies—took its toll. As the years passed, I was less and less fulfilled, felt underappreciated for my efforts, and mainly wanted to do something I had passion for that made a *real* difference in the world.

After 12 years, I got the "wake-up" call that many of us get when life is waiting for us to correct course. Nothing will get your attention more than your body breaking down! A cancer scare was what it took for me to hear from deep within, *"You created disease, and you can create health, and you are at a turning point. Next time you might not be so lucky."* It was time to change my life. I took a leap of faith, leaving an unhealthy relationship and my corporate job of 12 years to, in my eyes, "save my life."

My illness began my journey and passion for holistic well-being (physical, emotional, mental, and spiritual). Having previously been trained and certified as a personal trainer (for fun), it seemed like a great marriage to bring in life/wellness coaching. Once I was certified as a professional life coach, I pursued this passion and took on the lofty goal (and investment) to open a wellness center for women.

I went bankrupt and lost my home in less than two years. In hindsight, I realized that one of the main reasons the business failed was that, *although I had a passion for the wellness center, my true motivation for the business was tied more to achieving success and proving my value than to a deeper purpose*. Sure, I had passion, but it wasn't *the* work I was meant to do in the world. The work my whole life had been preparing me for deeply connected to my own greatest struggle and life's journey to know my value and purpose in the world.

My worst fears were realized. I had failed. After the business closed and I had gone bankrupt, my inability to support myself caused me to have to rely on others to support me financially—something that was very hard for me to accept, as I'd always been the "rock", the successful one. My health deteriorated due to chronic stress, resulting in adrenal fatigue, stomach issues, and chronic back pain. I felt like a failure and deeply questioned my own value. It took years to regain my self-confidence!

After the wellness center, I took my business "on the road," focusing strictly on the professional coaching. No more storefront. I was relieved, but I continued to struggle financially because of inconsistent revenue and clients. *In hindsight, I realized I was being a "generalist". I had no niche, no specific client/tribe with a specific problem that needed to be solved, and most importantly, no specific value (outcome) or bold promise that allowed people to raise their hands and say "I want that!"* To invest and commit to working with me because they had something that they desired to change—something they felt confident I could help them to resolve and achieve.

I would go to networking groups and find myself stumbling to articulate what I did, and I leaned heavily on referrals from others who had used my services. For years, I secretly cringed at the question, "What do you do?"— a question I have found most passion-driven entrepreneurs greatly struggle with. Don't get me wrong, referral business is awesome and, quite frankly, a great source of clients. However, when you as the service provider are unable to clearly articulate what you do, who you specifically serve, and the specific outcome that you can provide, why would you think that someone else could possibly convey that for you? The clients who worked with me were pleased, and they would tell others about their experience, so whatever I helped each individual client with was what they conveyed, and it was rarely the same outcome. This made it nearly impossible to be "known for something" and build a solid practice of clients and consistent revenue. Not just that, but your level of expertise in a given area does not really get honed as "a generalist."

Successful business owners know who they serve—their specific problems, greatest struggles, and the exact outcomes they are seeking. Period. What I've seen with passion-based business owners—because they have so much to offer and can help in so many ways—is that they resist being known for something because they are afraid they will exclude people or limit their success. Yet that is the very thing that keeps them struggling!

When I decided to get abundantly honest with myself about where I had breakthroughs, and also why I was still struggling in my business and life, my business took off. Why? Because in seeing my own challenges, giving myself credit for all the many ways I had actually transformed in these areas, and seeing where I was still "in progress" in an area, I was able to hone in specifically on the very ways I could help someone else powerfully make changes in their lives. I stood solidly and confidently in the value I had to offer, and I could see where I was not ready to step into teaching others yet. I identified my "sweet spot" that had immense value for clients, and by acknowledging the difference between the transformations I could support in others and those that I wasn't ready to teach yet, I was able to own my value, maintain high integrity, and have great confidence.

Further, when I realized I was struggling because I did not know who I was serving and that I was creating offers "in a bubble" (not knowing or asking my tribe what they wanted), I became a sleuth. With every opportunity I had of talking to and working with my tribe, I watched them like a hawk. I would look for where they were making progress and, most importantly, where they were, as a group, commonly getting "stuck" in moving forward. Where in their lives did they still struggle? From there, I became a problem solver extraordinaire. But I didn't do it in a bubble. I talked with them. I listened. I heard where they were struggling. I asked them what support they wanted. Over time, I got to see the common breakdowns and struggles and what was necessary for them to move forward at each phase.

This is where beauty resides: the place where your personal transformations and your tribe's greatest struggles and problems collide and align. This is where you will truly be in your purpose and passion! Imagine identifying a major transformation in your life and knowing with certainty that you could walk someone else through the very process you went through to meet this challenge (and it is a process—always), able to clearly articulate the problem, the greatest struggles you faced, and the transformation (result) you made. Ears will perk up; people with the exact same struggles and problems who desire the result you experienced will have to ask you, "How did you do it?" Imagine that you have a business designed specifically to solve their very challenges. You talk with them and know—I mean you *really* know—that you can help them. You hear their pain and struggle and recall it just like it was yesterday. Your heart is open, you truly want to support them, and you know how to engage in the conversation to inspire them to hire you. You take them through the process you went through, and the transformation they desire is realized. This is a purposeful business, and very rewarding!

To help you with the exercise to begin revealing your passion, here is a summary of the breakthroughs that I experienced and the transformation that shifted my purposeful business from struggle to success:

Identified my authentic passion and purpose: I realized my life's work (including my own evolutionary purpose) was about knowing one's value—valuing one's self and knowing our value in the world.

Identified the value I had to offer that aligned with this passion: I became very clear on how my life's purpose and personal experiences (from breakdowns to breakthroughs) had perfectly prepared me to support my tribe and that I had immense value to offer (while recognizing my transformational edge—where I was growing and evolving to the next level).

I got to really know my tribe and their greatest struggles and problems: I began really listening to and understanding my tribe, asking them directly what support they wanted, where they felt stuck, and connecting my transformations to the support I could provide them specifically to resolve their problems (bold promise).

Created a high-value program based upon my own transformation that I knew, with confidence, could deliver the specific outcome my tribe desired: I utilized my Vision process—how I was able to break through my struggles in business and create a purposeful business and program in alignment with *my* true desires and needs, one with a clear value that clients readily invested in and ensured the money and time that I wanted for my ideal life.

Learned how to powerfully articulate what I do and the value I offer to successfully enroll clients: I created a specific process for taking my tribe's greatest struggles and problems and the transformation my programs provided (Bold Promise) to confidently clarify and articulate what I do, who I serve, and the value that is received as a result of my programs. This process became the foundation of my Signature System and Big Reveal Program (deeply serving my purpose).

Clarified my "Big Why" and how it connects directly to my deeper purpose (life's work) to confidently step out into the world in a bigger way: I created a process for clarifying my life's passion and purpose and how my story directly connects to my tribe, emotionally inspiring those who want the same transformation to learn from me so they, too, can have a successful passion (purposeful) business. This process also became the foundation of my Signature System and Big Reveal Program.

An Exercise to Reveal and Draw Out Your Passion!

The following exercise will help you to begin the journey to revealing your passion (and possibly your life's purpose). This exercise, "Know Your Value and Purpose", is one of the steps used in my Big Reveal Program to create a business you love that supports you!

It's a fairly simple process, although if you allow yourself to "go deep", it can really take some time. The deeper you go, the more likely you are to reveal a true passion (and possibly purpose) that will become the foundation for your new business—where you will make the greatest impact helping support the people who really want and need it.

1. Write down the five most challenging times of your life. Simply ask yourself, "When did I really have a hard time in my life?" For an example, refer back to my story and "breakthroughs."

2. Now that you have the breakdowns listed, return to each of them. Underneath, list all the ways that you managed to break through these challenging times in your life. It doesn't mean you won't have challenges in this area ever again, but simply that you have experienced transformation—which is a lifelong process—and that you now have tools and processes that bring you back to the outcome you desire. Refer back to my story for examples.

3. Having difficulty identifying five challenging times of your own? You may also consider any struggles, challenges, or fears you may have witnessed in your family members or close friends—challenges that stayed with you particularly and may be bringing out a passion in your life.

   We are simply looking at the ways in which your life experiences (challenges, breakdowns, evolution, healing, triumphs, and transformations) have elicited a deeper passion and purpose, preparing you to have immense value and the ability to support others in an area of great demand. Consider what "pain" you may have experienced that provides you with the direct insights and ability to relate to your ideal client (someone just like you) and have the direct experience and knowledge to support their desired transformation, healing, growth, and/or outcome.

   Great Job!

4. Now take notice in your life: where are you already naturally seeking, studying, and passionate about the topics that are being revealed in your breakdowns and breakthroughs? Look for a natural connection to what you do (or seek) *and* the transformation, growth, and successes

that you have personally experienced in your life.

It is time to own the value you have to offer others and really ask yourself, "What am I passionate about, and who am I passionate about helping?" When you look at what you've been able to transform in your own life, ask yourself, "Do I have a passion for helping others in any of these areas?"

Congratulations! You may have just revealed your passion (and possibly your life's purpose). Please know that it takes time and experience, working with your tribe and your own ongoing transformations, to deepen the awareness of your passion and purpose, the outcomes they desire, and the value you can boldly and confidently offer.

This is how you lay the foundation for a successful passion-based (purposeful) business that has immense value to the people you are meant to serve!

ABOUT DEBBY

Debby is the founder of Niche On Purpose, and with her exclusive Big Reveal Program specializes in supporting women in passion-driven businesses to articulate what they do, the value they offer to the world, and their "Why" Story that reaches and compels their ideal clients to work with them.

Debby has more than over 15 years' experience as an entrepreneur: as the CEO and founder of Vibrant Lady Health & Fitness, the founder of Niche on Purpose, and a professional coach for SSI and EIS Consulting.

Her corporate experience provides a strong analytical, systematic, and organized perspective, and her visionary gifts provide a powerful, creative, and intuitive insight for aligning and living true to oneself and fulfilling your deeper calling in an established business structure. Debby's intuitive gifts allow her to see her client's paths more fully, enabling her to guide them through letting go of the path that is not serving them and moving them powerfully into their passion life and work. Learn more: www.DebbyEubank.com.

LEAN OUT MOMENT

Vivian Sayward

I've been on the business side of the biotechnology and pharmaceutical industry since 1988. My flight from corporate life was more of a process than a moment.

I had a lucrative career as the director of Drug Delivery, Biotechnology Division for Sicor, a sizable company based out of Italy. I was living in Southern California, but I'm originally from New York. I lost a close friend in the tragedy of 9/11, which certainly sent me on a mission to reevaluate everything in my life. It was a wake-up call, to say the least. At that point, I had been in my career for over a decade and knew it was time to spread my wings. Only a few months later, I left the corporate nest to explore building something of my own.

Like many, I started with the foundational knowledge I'd gained throughout my career and began consulting with small life-science companies—primarily in market research and business development. I enjoyed the flexibility that consulting gave me, but after a while, I longed to dig in and create something.

After consulting for more than six years, I had an opportunity to work with a friend who was launching a women's fitness line, an area I've always been passionate about. While that partnership wasn't a "perfect marriage", it gave me a foothold in the industry and eventually led me to launch my own line of women's activewear—www.VivacitySportswear.com—which is manufactured in California and sold all over the country.

My decade in corporate was an important part of the journey. I always made it a point to stay in touch with prior colleagues and mentors. In fact, this is what ultimately led me to that "perfect marriage", as I ended up marrying a wonderful man I had worked with at Sicor years before!

ABOUT

Vivian Sayward is founder and CEO of Vivacity Sportswear, a high-end sportswear line designed for and by women and produced in Southern California. The company was established in 2011, and its collection is carried in golf pro shops, resorts, and boutiques across the US. The collection combines sport with haute couture; head-turning silhouettes with everyday comfort; and refined detailing with wicking, antimicrobial fabrics. www.VivacitySportswear.com

Chapter 8
Strengths

WHILE I DISCOVERED SOME of my strengths at an early age, others took time to reveal themselves. That is why launching Hera Hub was so important to me—it was the magic moment when my passions and strengths aligned. It allowed me to create my own utopia where I could build a strong platform for myself and others to lead, collaborate, inspire, share, build, and flourish.

One of the most well-known assessments for finding one's strengths is *StrengthsFinder 2.0*. Created by the Gallup organization and based on the research of Dr. Donald Clifton, *StrengthsFinder 2.0* is a book by Tom Rath. Rath argues that from "cradle to cubicle", the vast majority of people are unfulfilled in their careers because they are not in positions that best leverage their strengths.

I've taken the StrengthsFinder assessment several times. My top five are:

> ***Futuristic***—*People strong in the Futuristic theme are inspired by the future and what could be. They inspire others with their visions of the future.*
>
> ***Self-Assurance***—*People strong in the Self-assurance theme feel confident in their ability to manage their own lives. They possess an inner compass that gives them confidence that their decisions are right.*
>
> ***Strategic***—*People strong in the Strategic theme create alternative ways to proceed. Faced with any given scenario, they can quickly spot the relevant patterns and issues.*

Belief—*People strong in the Belief theme have certain core values that are unchanging. Out of these values emerges a defined purpose for their life.*

Responsibility—*People strong in the Responsibility theme take psychological ownership of what they say they will do. They are committed to stable values such as honesty and loyalty.*

Also, in my top ten are:

Positivity—*People strong in the Positivity theme have an enthusiasm that is contagious. They are upbeat and can get others excited about what they are going to do.*

Maximizer—*People strong in the Maximizer theme focus on strengths as a way to stimulate personal and group excellence. They seek to transform something strong into something superb.*

Connectedness—*People strong in the Connectedness theme have faith in the links between all things. They believe there are few coincidences and that almost every event has a reason.*

Diplomacy is a strength that I've recently come to recognize in myself (although I'm not sure if that is in the 34 StrengthsFinder themes). I love using this strength to ensure everyone in a group is heard and to gently guide them to consensus—perhaps a skill that I'll use more and more as I grow Hera Hub.

As popular as it is, the *StrengthsFinder* assessment has been criticized by some as arbitrary, incomplete, and unbalanced. That is why I particularly enjoyed the contribution from Hera Hub member, MaryCay Durrant. She took a different approach to finding one's strengths, and she also used the flight analogy. As you will see, MaryCay provides her analogy of flight through the theme of development, and the beautiful transformation a butterfly undergoes.

MaryCay Durrant - Let The Evolution Begin

Do you ever feel like a burdened bug, slugging your way through workdays filled with other people's priorities, wishing that you had wings to soar, doing work you love? Excellent. Join me in exploring how nature's mysteries hold the unique formula for each of us to fulfill our heart's desires.

We can see this clearly by looking at caterpillars' "imaginal cells", which contain the blueprint for the butterfly they have the potential to become. Even the name sounds like "imagination", which is elemental to how we create as human beings. And just like the wings are already inside the caterpillar, our strengths and values are our "imaginal cells", ready to guide our journey from daily drudgery to shining light.

In my late 30s, having landed a "spectacular" opportunity to drive cultural integration on an international scale, my weeks were a series of fast-paced business trips, compelling growth strategies, and large-scale projects. Life should have been great; this was what guidance counselors and adults had steered me toward since my first high school aptitude test. I was living the American dream, and yet something wasn't quite what I'd expected.

I woke up in Sydney Australia, shut off my alarm, and pressed the bedside button that silently peeled back the blinds to reveal a serene harbor beckoning my eyes towards the famous opera house, a glistening lotus lit by morning sun. I burst into tears. I was someplace I had always dreamed of seeing, and I was holed up in a generically opulent hotel room working on PowerPoint presentations and project plans for the next day, which would be spent in an equally generic conference room talking synergies and growth projections with the senior leaders from a recently acquired business. I was tired. I felt like a fraud. I ate a cookie in a failed attempt to make myself feel a little better and slogged through another day.

I told myself that maybe it was jet lag because, truth be told, I was inspired by the people on the trip with me: the CEO who was both mentor and boss as well as the savvy, brilliant, and fun executives. Yet, at some unspoken level in my being, I knew I was not passionate about the work in front of me. It bored me and gave me anxiety in the same minute. How is that even possible? Something that bores me should put me to sleep versus causing me to feel tense and anxious. I felt like Rudolph without a red nose to show me the way; I was a misfit in this world of people who seemed quite taken with shareholder value and quarterly results.

That moment stayed with me for months, haunting my commute at the end of long days drained of the spirit to be playful, kind, and happy. Forget about enjoying an adventure, such as that trip to Sydney—I was too busy slogging through the endless list of someone else's to-dos.

During those reflective moments, I began to realize that I had swapped my dreams of being a teacher, adventurer, and writer for financial security, fitting in, and being perceived well by others. I'd traded my life energy and passion for promotions, bonuses, and external symbols of success. I looked at all I'd collected and said, "I thought this would make me happy, and it hasn't; now it's time for something new."

Pondering my plight, I began a seven-year journey to let go of all the "shoulds" that I'd layered so deeply into my life that it was hard to see where I was behind the cheery façade that showed up for work every day. Often, below the seemingly sunny surface seethed resentment and frustration that I was only subconsciously aware I was suppressing. The expectations of performing, pleasing authority, being "nice," and fitting in had center stage. The process of reclaiming myself and creating a thriving business was murky and scary, especially since it required tugging off the security blanket of "stable income" and learning to believe in myself. Going back to the caterpillar, this time was my cocoon, a messy and necessary part of the process. I wouldn't trade one second of the muddy, messy journey for the beat-down, tired, numb, exhausted, "this can't really be my life" experience I'd been enduring.

For inspiration, I turn always to nature. Seasonal patterns create a flow for growth in the natural world. I've adopted a similar approach for my continued growth and vitality. This cycle gives structure to my expansion in much the same way the cocooning process supports the caterpillar. This process also gives me some peace in the "messy middle" when the going gets tough:

- Clearing is about pruning away what no longer serves me and tending to what is mine to either heal and release or feed and grow.
- Connecting to life through my values, strengths, and passions, which require learning to honor what I need, no matter how it looks to others.

Connecting is also about embracing collaboration where, in the past, I might have felt there was competition. This in itself has been life changing, requiring me to move beyond limiting beliefs about myself and the way the world—business and otherwise—truly works. I remind myself regularly that the sequoia trees, one of my favorite symbols of strength, intertwine their roots with one another to thrive. In nature and in business, those who have the tools for partnership, and can distinguish true collaboration versus competition, flourish.

- o Creating is simply engaging and taking the next step. I remind myself that the angel of illumination only shows one step in front of us at a time, and this is a blessing, even if we may not think so in the moment. It's also about realizing that birth of all kind is messy and requires embracing failure and play, both of which accelerate the process of growth—whether it's an idea, a product, or a sense of who we are. This is how I built the "runway" that would allow me to soar vs. stumble when I first left the corporate world.
- o Celebrating is pausing along the way to relish and receive; it's the warm sunshine that gives me the energy to keep going through the parts that are hard work.

Our strengths and values are the DNA for a thriving life—our own personal "imaginal cells". They are gifts from the universe pointing us in the direction of prosperity and sustainable happiness. When we live in our strengths, we have a sense of vitality, flow, and power. We flourish in ways we cannot imagine inside the paradigm of working hard and surviving. Strengths are not simply things we are good at; they are the things that make us feel good. Contrast my experience doing work I was good at—project management, which made me feel exhausted—with work that makes me feel good—creating business cultures that thrive by bringing out the best in everyone.

Just as our strengths are the seeds of greatness, weaknesses are the soil that nurtures growth. Like soil, they can seem dark and dense, but they are rich in nutrients and they show us where we need to create empowering partnerships to have the full potential of our dream realized.

When we pause and open our awareness, we see an abundance of mutual benefit woven richly into every breath of life. Simply noticing the way bees effortlessly pollinate fruit while gathering nectar for honey shows us a roadmap to thrive ourselves. This collaboration in nature illuminates that when we clear and own "our part" of the partnership, that activity naturally leads to growth and value.

We are designed the same way; our strength shows us our part. Our weaknesses show us where to find others for collaboration. When we find partners that are a "fit", our values and purpose intertwine, and we all thrive, enhancing our experience, energy, and vitality. This actually gives us even greater capacity to create ever more value in the areas of our purpose and passion. It's like our own renewable energy source! In this way, we get to shine and not be exhausted by doing things that are not ours to do. It's as spectacular, beautiful, and graceful as a sunrise.

As a side note, our weaknesses are different from derailers, which are old patterns we've taken on from our family or culture that no longer serve us. These derailers are in our blind spots and represent an area where collaboration can turn risks into areas of strength, in the same way that fire burns away weakness and strengthens the sequoia so it can grow more quickly for up to 100 years after the burn.

When I started my journey to living my strengths, I needed to start at the very beginning, which was realizing that I was giving my spirit away to other people's priorities. I needed to clear out the gunk I'd taken on that wasn't my essence. I hardly knew where to begin. About this same time, I was enjoying an unseasonably warm spring day in the

Midwest. While watering my flowers, I noticed a chubby caterpillar munching on my freshly potted plants. I wondered, "Might it be possible that there is a butterfly inside of me, ready to burst forth?"

Shortly after that fateful spring morning, I did an exercise that helped me rediscover my true strengths, my own "imaginal cells". Like the caterpillar, I didn't instantly turn into a butterfly, but finding and honoring my strengths was an important first step in the process. If you are like me, you may find this exercise provides access to embracing and nurturing your strengths, your unique-in-all-time-and-space "imaginal cells". In remembering what is uniquely ours to bring forth in the world, we also recovery the ability to believe in ourselves and the beauty of our dreams.

An Exercise In Evolution

Here is a pragmatic exercise to help us discover how we can transform from the caterpillar we've been living as to the butterfly we are meant to evolve into:

Spend a few weeks noticing when you feel most alive or seem to lose track of time. Note when you feel happy, playful, or even decadent. Pause. *Write whatever you notice on a slip of paper and stick that paper in a jar to be set aside.*

Over this same period of time, select six to ten people to interview. Trust the same intelligence that grows your fingernails and teaches the dolphins to swim to point you towards the people who will give you the greatest insights.

Questions are fateful. They determine destinations. They are the chamber through which destiny calls.

– Godwin Hlatshwayo

If you want a great life, ask great questions, and then explore, wonder, and play in the inquiry of great answers. It all starts with the questions we ask ourselves *and others*:

1. What are my strengths?
2. What are my weaknesses?
3. What do you/can you count on me for? What can others count on me for?
4. What is something that you wish I embraced about myself?
5. What do you think might hold me back from achieving my dreams?
6. Who am I to you?
7. How do I contribute to your life? To life itself?

If this is too many, I would pull the "who am I to you" question—it's often the most difficult to answer.

When you conduct the interviews, record what people share. During this time, continue to notice moments of strength and vitality; write those insights on slips of paper and put them in the same jar.

At the end of all the interviews, sift through all the slips of paper and the interview notes. Notice the themes that emerge and how they make you feel.

This process is not like a sixth-grade algebra equation where there is only one right answer. It's more like sitting around a campfire watching the stars come out at night. At first they are dim and seem very distant, but over time, with patience, the whole sky fills with twinkling lights of immense power that fill us with wonder and possibility. Our strengths and values are like the vast night sky, waiting for us to see them and tap into their power.

Are you ready to live a life as vast as the Milky Way? Are you willing to live as the person described in the interviews and slips of paper? If so, you are ready to embrace your natural strengths and create a values-centered business and life.

Embracing My Strengths On The Journey To My Own Business

When I look back now, I realize that if I'd tried to jump right from the frying pan (a.k.a., the corporate world) into the fire (entrepreneur) without first practicing my newly "imagined" self inside my current life, I would have brought some of my old patterns with me and unconsciously recreated them in my own business.

To illustrate, let's go back to the caterpillar and its metamorphosis. The caterpillar doesn't go to sleep one cool spring night and wake up the next morning a butterfly. There's a messy metamorphosis in the middle. During this process, the caterpillar does a lot of work—spinning a cocoon, using all its energy to create a safe space and then turning into a sea of goo. Think about that—it must be pretty uncomfortable (and maybe even scary) to become a blob of goo, give up all that you've known yourself to be, and trust those darn "imaginal cells" to transform your very essence. Yet that is just what caterpillars do every spring. These special cells, the blueprint of the possibility, feed on the goo of the caterpillar to bring forth the butterfly. The beating of the wings against the cocoon wall, while painful to watch (as I remember vividly from my youth), is a critical step in building enough strength to fly, plus it removes the goo remnants still clinging onto the caterpillar. I would cry, watching the butterfly struggle, and my mom would say over and over again, "It has to do this or it will die. It's building the strength it needs to fly."

It turned out that the same was true for me. This gift from nature mirrors my own journey from corporate slug to entrepreneurial butterfly. Have you experienced the beating of your wings against the cocoon of your current life? If not, know that it is a necessary part of the journey. Like the butterfly, we need to do the work ourselves. My Dad always said to me, "You have to spade your own garden, MaryCay."

Yet it is not meant to be a solo journey. Early on in the metamorphosis process, the caterpillar's immune system tries to kill of the "imaginal cells." These cells of the future strengthen themselves by finding each other and bonding together. Like the "imaginal" cells, we benefit greatly from having others around us who believe in us through this process.

I will be forever grateful to the people who were my "imaginal cells". They helped me bring perspective to my own growth—to see my strengths emerging— and encouraged me to pick myself up and be kind to myself after a particularly messy attempt at practicing my commitments.

As I began to discover my strengths and values and practice them inside the "container" of my corporate job, this gave me several benefits. First, I got to practice blending kindness and results in an environment that was all about assessment and what-have-you-done-for-me-lately. I practiced openness, inclusiveness, and collaboration inside an environment focused on producing more results with less. So much of what I was practicing seemed opposite to the environment itself—and yet this was the perfect place to "strengthen my strengths" to prepare myself to fly. This was my cocoon, a place to discover and strengthen my "imaginal cells" and begin the messy transformation.

The other benefit this time had was that it gave me a runway to untangle my life and financial commitments. Small businesses that succeed are those that have money left after their first round of learning to pivot and keep going, so this practice time inside the corporate structure provided many benefits. First, it let me contribute something I valued to the organization while I was still there, enabling me to leave with my dignity and honor intact because I'd been congruent with my authentic self at the end. Second, it gave me the opportunity to clarify and strengthen my purpose before launching on my own. Finally, it gave me the time to set up a financial runway long enough that I had room for failure and learning in my new venture. This trifecta proved immensely valuable in keeping me from going into a scarcity fear mindset in my new business; that in itself contributed immensely to my success.

On reflection, most of all, I'd like to thank each of those wise, courageous, and honorable people who helped me along this journey. They truly are the greatest gift of nature and the most important ingredient in supporting the journey to the freedom to soar.

ABOUT MARYCAY

MaryCay Durrant guides executive leaders and transforms business-as-usual with her unique blend of pragmatic business savvy and neuroscience-based communication models that ignite energy and accelerate business performance.

Culling from her extensive experience in talent and leadership development in the Fortune 50 world, MaryCay speaks and facilitates learning for companies, organizations and conferences on the topics of Values-Centered Leadership, Working in Partnership, Diversity & Inclusion, Leading Naturally for Real Value and Igniting Human Spirit. She is the co-founder of BON.FIRE, a business leadership company enriching business performance by supporting women executives and business owners to enliven their organizations.

MaryCay cherishes her extended family and adventures. She lives in San Diego with her husband Michael and pets Sequoia and Patches.

Learn more at www.MaryCayDurrant.com

LEAN OUT MOMENT

Stephanie San Antonio

While still in college, I took on a part-time position in marketing and administration with Keith Eck Financial (founded by a former NFL player). I'm a very outgoing person, so I quickly longed to get out from behind a desk and have more client interaction. Over the course of ten years, I spearheaded and grew a robust employee benefits arm for Keith's financial-planning firm.

While I appreciated all the mentorship and support Keith provided me, my entrepreneurial genes began to kick in (my Dad has owned a marina all my life). As I approached my 30th birthday, I started to look at my options for career growth. I was approached by a few employee benefit companies, but in my heart I knew I wanted to create my own brand and have a real impact.

I decided to hire a business coach, I knew through my

network, to help me map out my exit. She also helped me with accountability and reminded me that "I could do this!" It gave me a tremendous amount of confidence to move forward and approach Keith about buying him out and taking my clients with me. I wanted to make sure I left with a solid foundation, able to leave the firm on good terms and take my client relationships with me. We struck a deal, and I set out to launch SSA Insurance Services at age 31.

ABOUT

Stephanie is the founder of SSA Insurance Services, which develops custom benefits solutions that fit within a company's philosophy, meet budget guidelines, and relieve the company of the time and liability associated with performing critical and time-consuming benefits administration. Their expertise and access to major providers and carriers allow them to negotiate on the client's behalf and provide them with many options.

www.SSAInsuranceServices.com

Chapter 9
Vision

SINCE *VISIONARY* IS IN my top five strengths, this is one of my favorite parts of taking flight. I admittedly sometimes live in the clouds. However, I routinely try to live in the moment and be present.

I've created several vision boards over the years. My divorce from Brian, around the age of 30, was the catalyst for mapping a new life-path. I spent a quiet Saturday night home by myself with a stack of magazines and a glass of wine. Of course, I turned on inspirational music and lit candles to set the mood.

Over the course of the next four hours, my first masterpiece emerged. It included quintessential pictures of tropical islands and lovers embracing affectionately. I remember struggling when it came to putting a picture of children on the board. Did I want children? Unlike many women my age, I wasn't sensitive to my "ticking clock." I decided that I did want some semblance of family, so I found a picture of a grade-school-aged, brown-bushy-haired boy running down a sunlit beach. To this day, that image is still etched in my mind.

After Brian, I dated the wrong guy for two and a half years. Okay, let's call it out for what it was—a long rebound! When I jumped back into the dating pool again, it wasn't long until I met Keith. On our fourth or fifth date, I met his son Kyle. Wouldn't you know, he was eight years old and had brown, bushy hair. Be careful what you wish for!

Ready To Create Your Vision

I met Lorin Beller Blake through Linda Lattimore (also a Texas girl). Lorin joined Hera Hub when she moved to San Diego and led a Business Booster session in early 2014. As with the other exercises, I strongly encourage you to take the time to create your vision. At the end of this section I will share the vision I created in my session with Lorin.

Lorin Beller Blake - Beyond Vision

Woodrow Wilson said it best: "You are not here merely to make a living. You are here in order to enable the world to live more amply, with greater vision, with a finer spirit of hope and achievement. You are here to enrich the world, and you impoverish yourself if you forget the errand."

From working the past 14 years as a business coach and consultant, supporting thousands of female entrepreneurs in realizing their vision, I have come to know that your vision is the most valuable business tool you have. I also have come to believe, at my core, that your vision is possible.

Did you hear that? *Your vision is possible.*

I have been witness to women who have pulled themselves up by their bootstraps and created wild success. I have been witness to women who had to get very bold and ask for what they wanted from the world around them. I have been witness to women who have had their power shut off because they couldn't pay the power bill and then created a lifestyle that allowed them to travel 12 weeks per year now. I have been witness to women who lost their husbands, then their businesses—then created an extraordinary life.

Here is what I know: your vision is like your fingerprint, like no other. Your vision is unique, and all visions (when truly authentic) are created only with love. They have truly good intent, and that is good for the world. Your vision matters. Your vision, in action, changes the world.

How do you develop your vision? There is no reason to develop it. It is inside of you. It just needs you to give it a bit of attention. You need to capture it and pull it out of you in order to get conscious about it.

Defining your Vision Exercise

Here is a powerful exercise that will help you better define your vision:

Make yourself ten years older than you are today. Write a letter to someone (of your choice) from that older, wiser perspective about where you are, what impact you've had in the world, and what you learned along the way to have that impact. This letter can be written to a child or parent (ten years older than they are today), or perhaps someone close to you who is no longer living, but you choose the person that you will share your vision with.

This written vision should be palpable; you *should* have emotion when you read it. Feelings make this tool have its value.

The aim of the exercise is to give you a tool that helps you feel where you want to end up. Feelings matter and help guide this process.

Once you write your vision, ask yourself: "If I do not follow through on my vision, what do I rob the world of? What is possible when I realize my vision? What is the ripple effect of following my vision?"

As you write, what you are writing about is *not* the "how" you got there; more importantly, you are writing about the impact you have had in the world. You are writing about that moment in time and where you are in aspects of your life:

health, relationships, your impact on your community, your happiness, etc. You want to stay away from material things and extravagance. Get clear on what you truly love at your core and what you want your life to be filled with at that time and stage of your life.

This process is not something to agonize over. Instead, it is a process that should take no more than 30 minutes and be no longer than one full handwritten page. It is in letter format. It is you projecting out ten years and being witness to what and who you have become and, because of that, the impact you have had in the world.

Take the time to write. Now.

Once your vision is written, the next step is to make a commitment to it. A commitment like you've never made before. A vision cannot happen without a commitment to it. Create a little ceremony for yourself. The ceremony may be that you put it in a pretty envelope, you read it to someone close to you, or you send it to this contributing author (see note at end of chapter), but when you do that, you say the following words (or something like it):

"I, (your name), am committed to seeing this vision through. I keep my attention on it on a regular basis, which means I reread it as often as I need to keep my focus. When I get stuck, I speak to someone who helps me get in action again. If I get discouraged, I acknowledge that it is just a bump in my road and try to learn from the bump as best as I can so that I can get in action and move toward this vision. My vision matters. I matter, because I am the leader of my vision."

The next step is to know that a vision also cannot happen without faith—faith and trust in yourself. Trust that you can do it. These two things, commitment and faith, are needed over and over again. Commitment keeps you moving forward. Faith is what you need when you get weary.

I like to think of vision, commitment, and faith as the three strands of a braid. In order to reach your vision, you need all three components. You need to keep your eye on your vision at all times. You need the commitment to it so when it gets tough you keep taking one step toward it. And you need faith (trust) in yourself that you will follow through and that your vision is worth it. These three components are like the three strands of a braid.

What I have also seen is that when we make a commitment to ourselves and we do not follow through, we hinder our own self-confidence. On the other hand, when we make a commitment to ourselves and follow through (on whatever it is) we become more self-confident. Self-confidence creates more self-confidence.

Another important point is that when our vision is crystal clear and we have made a 100-percent commitment to it, miracles happen. Do not worry about how you will create your vision. First, just design your vision (end game) and free yourself from the "how" of it. The "how" are goals, which is a whole different chapter! From the place of the clear vision, the "how" will show up, and sometimes we have no idea what that will look like. What I also know is that when we begin to move toward the vision and implement what looks like that first step toward the vision, we learn, and as we learn, we see the next step that we would not have seen without the first step.

About 12 years ago, I was working with a client. She had a full-time job. She was launching her massage practice. She said that what would be perfect would be if she could cut her full-time job (where she was a rock star and received full health benefits) back to a part-time job with full-time benefits. She thought her boss would never let her do that. We brainstormed, and she got up the courage to ask her boss for what she wanted. She was shocked: he agreed to what she wanted and more! She was on her way to building that new massage practice. Sometimes our version of the "how" will get in the way of creating our vision if our vision is not clear enough or our commitment to the vision is not strong enough.

I have personally created a lifestyle that allows me to volunteer in my daughter's classroom and have quality time with her after school, and it still affords me an income that covers my SoCal lifestyle and my second home in New York. If I can do that, so can you. I have no special talents or tools. They are the same ones that you have. I was raised in a blue-collar home, and my mother was a stay-at-home mom. I do have to say that I think that our Western culture is causing us more stress because of our need to compare our earnings and wealth and material things with others. It has us thinking that bigger is better and more is the goal, but what I have come to know is that in my vision, today, what is most important are my relationships with those I love, a simple lifestyle, and making a positive difference every day. That is what truly matters. When we stop chasing society's version of what we think we should do, life miraculously works with us in creating our vision. I am not suggesting you make your vision smaller; I am suggesting you get extremely clear about what you want at your deepest core.

Our world needs more people to follow their vision. Our world needs more people to stay true to themselves. Our world needs more people to be truly happy inside. The way to change the world is by starting in our own homes. To walk our talk. To create your vision, then live it daily, fully. That is how we change the world together. But we each have a responsibility and a part. Don't forget your errand.

Tell me what you plan to do with your one wild and precious life.

– Mary Oliver

If, after reading this chapter, you write your vision, make a commitment to it, and want to share it with the contributing author, Lorin, she welcomes your communication. Please email her at Lorin@LorinBeller.com.

ABOUT LORIN

Lorin Beller is a business coach who has been working with women entrepreneurs since 2001. She is an international speaker, speaking to thousands of women via women entrepreneur organizations all across North America. She was a successful entrepreneur herself prior to becoming a business coach. She, with a partner, started a technology firm in the early '90s, grew it quickly to a $3 million firm, and sold it. Since then, she has worked with women entrepreneurs from coast to coast in assisting, strategizing, inspiring, supporting, and maintaining accountability on the journey for hundreds of women entrepreneurs over the years. It is truly her passion and her life's work, aside from raising her strong and heart-centered daughter. Lorin and her daughter live in Southern California, and she has a vacation home in upstate New York where she hosts her women's retreats. Learn more at www.LorinBeller.com.

Now... here is my vision!

March 2025

As I sit on the beach in St. John, after an amazing five-mile run, I reflect on how much has happened over the last ten years. I feel blessed to have had an opportunity to support more than a million women in their "flight to freedom"—business launch and growth via the Hera Hub family. I remain on the Hera Hub leadership team but have stepped out of the day-to-day operations to tackle the world of higher education, changing the way we teach business in more than 1000 schools. I'm proud to say my work has inspired the next generation to become entrepreneurs, returning our society to its roots of independence and accountability. My word: IMPACT

Parting Thoughts For Your Upcoming Journey

My biggest piece of advice is to take time to find where your passion and strengths intersect with market need, (your sweet spot) and then dig in. Build a strong vision—both written and visual. Spend time refining the market need and target market, and move diligently towards setting clear goals—this will come with time.

I hope you've found these stories and exercises helpful in crafting your "lean out" strategy.

Now it's your turn to write your next chapter! How will you unleash your inner rebel, solidify your reinvention, and thrive?

For videos and additional content go to www.FlightClubBook.com

Part Four

Flight Notes

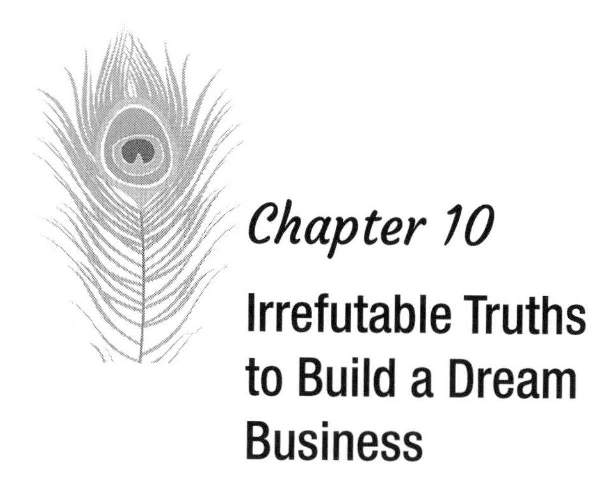

Chapter 10

Irrefutable Truths to Build a Dream Business

HOW ARE YOU FEELING? I hope the prior exercises and stories given you the base you need to move towards your dream business! As you get ready to take flight, I want to share a few final thoughts and tips. These are things I've learned throughout my entrepreneurial journey.

Finally, I would also like to add a tribute to my muse, Astrid Hanson (aka Grandma) and a note about my great grandma Felena.

Passion Will Carry You Through

As Sara Clark-Williams and Debby Eubank described so well, don't start a business just to make money. Yes, you're in charge of your time and have full choice in what you do and how you do it (unless it involves government regulations), but you will potentially work much harder than you did as an employee. If you're passionate about what you're doing, it will get you through the hard times.

> *Never give up on something that you can't go a day without thinking about.*
>
> ***– Winston Churchill***

Be Imperfect

As Voltaire famously wrote, "Le mieux est l'ennemi du bien"—the perfect is the enemy of the good. You will paralyze yourself if you insist that everything has to be perfect before your launch your business. That's why I love the "Lean" business methodology (Lean Business Canvas as outlined in the next section) —because it encourages you to test as you launch versus waiting to unveil your masterpiece.

> *Why, when we know that there's no such thing as perfect, do most of us spend an incredible amount of time and energy trying to be everything to everyone? Is it that we really admire perfection? No—the truth is that we are actually drawn to people who are real and down-to-earth. We love authenticity and we know that life is messy and imperfect.*
>
> ***– Brene Brown***

You'll Never Have It All Figured Out

Similar to the last point, business is not a "set it up and press cruise control" kind of venture—things are going to go "off course." At Hera Hub we try not to use the word "failure." I personally like the phrase "learning moment" (coined by the founder of WD-40, Gary Ridge) or the ever-popular "pivoting." Whatever you call it, you will always be learning and pivoting. That's just part of business! Yes, you need to plan, but be aware that it's going to shift.

> *I have not failed. I've just found 10,000 ways that won't work.*
>
> ***– Thomas A. Edison***

Determination

Business is hard. Yes, anything is possible, ***but*** you are going to have to be willing to stay the course (even if there are pivots along the way). There will be long hours and lots of frustration. Some days you'll feel like someone has socked you in the stomach—or, as Gary Vaynerchuk says, "punched you in the face." There will be many highs and many more lows. You must accept this and let your passion pull you through.

> *Nothing in this world can take the place of persistence. Talent will not; nothing is more common than unsuccessful men with talent. Genius will not; unrewarded genius is almost a proverb. Education will not; the world is full of educated derelicts. Persistence and determination alone are omnipotent. The slogan "Press On!" has solved and always will solve the problems of the human race.*
>
> ***– Calvin Coolidge***

Be Scrappy

Entrepreneurship is all about bootstrapping. You must do all you can to be resourceful and find ways to save money whenever possible. There are things you're going to have to learn to do yourself that you may have had an assistant take care of when you had a J-O-B.

This also means that if you're used to getting weekly manicures and eating out seven days a week, you may need to think about how you can cut down on these until you get things flowing again. I'm not suggesting that you think from a scarcity mindset, but be smart about the money you're spending. Ask, "Is this necessary right now?"

Finally, this also means you will, from time to time, have to fight. There have been many times when a building landlord or a vendor has tried to take advantage of a situation by overbilling me or not returning a deposit. You have to stand up for yourself, and yes, it might be uncomfortable, but that's part of doing business.

> *Fear is the disease. Hustle is the antidote.*
>
> ***– Travis Kalanick, co-founder of Uber***

Set Boundaries

You need to understand that you are not your business. I see this often when someone is consulting or providing a service—they have a difficult time not feeling personally hurt when someone doesn't accept a proposal or gives them a bad review. Men are much, much better at this. They compartmentalize things, while women mix everything up into one big plate of spaghetti! ***Do not***—I repeat, ***do not***—take things personally! Business is business. Get up, brush yourself off, and move on.

This also relates to "scope creep" for those service providers. For example, a month or two into the project, the client starts asking for more than what was included in the original agreement. You say to yourself, "Oh, that's just a small task, I'll just do it and not charge for it." That can add up quickly. Suddenly you're doing twice the amount of work than was agreed on and not being paid a penny more! Set boundaries. Have a conversation with the client early and often.

How people treat you is their karma; how you react is yours.
– Wayne Dyer

Watch Out For "Shiny Object Syndrome"

In today's world of constant bombardment, it's easy to be pulled off track. Everyone will try to give you advice, whether you want it or not. This will be challenging for you if 1) don't have a solid business plan and 2) you are not confident in your direction. Women are natural people pleasers. On top of that, they are often more sensitive to the thoughts and feelings of others. I've seen one comment send an entrepreneur on a completely different course.

Success is what happens after you have survived all your mistakes. – Anora Lee

Keep focused on your core business, and don't let the dozens of other ideas that come your way pull you too far off track. I recommend getting an idea journal or using a platform like Trello to note down all of those "great ideas" and "advice." After you have a solid foundation for your business, then you can go back and explore some of these ideas.

> *Focusing is about saying no.*
>
> **– Steve Jobs**

Be Sincerely Interested In Others

I always start out my introductions with "tell me about you" versus "what do you do?" People fascinate me—I'm sincerely interested in who they are and what makes them tick. I also work very hard to remember their name and something interesting about them. This is often surprising to people when I meet them a second time, and in turn, makes me memorable.

Tip: I do three things to remember someone's name:

1. *I'm a very visual person, so I try to get a glance at their nametag if they have one.*
2. *I immediately associate their name with someone I know who has the same name—it could be a cousin, a neighbor, or someone from college.*
3. *I use it as much as possible in our conversation—"Tell me about you, Diana," "Are you from San Diego, Diana?"*

Trust Your Instinct

Here is one of many places women have an advantage over men in business. We, for the most part, are willing to listen to our intuition. When I meet someone for the first time, I carefully listen and observe. I try to ask as many questions as possible and watch their body language. When my gut says, "something doesn't add up," it usually doesn't.

Sure, there have been times when the alarm went off in the back of my head and I ignored them. I tried to rationalize the situation, making excuses for the person. It has always come back to bite me. As I get older, my BS meter gets stronger, and I do my best to listen and act accordingly.

Follow your instincts. That's where true wisdom manifests itself.
– Oprah Winfrey

Follow Through

This is one of my biggest pet peeves. People say they are going to follow up—call you, e-mail you, etc., and they don't. I put people in two camps: those who keep their word and those who don't. For me, this is analogous to "integrity." I'm by far not the smartest person in the room, but because I do everything in my power to keep my word I've been able to build great relationships. Plus, it just feels good to do what you say you're going to do!

It was character that got us out of bed, commitment that moved us into action, and discipline that enabled us to follow through.
– Zig Ziglar

Stay Clear Of "Get Rich Quick" Schemes

Call it social selling, networking marketing, or multilevel marketing (MLM)—the concept of selling to your friends and family has been around for many years. It seems to have gained even more popularity after the recession, and especially among women. These companies sell the dream of "work from home, part-time, while simply educating your community about great products. Then get your friends and family to join you in saving the world and you'll all get rich." Sounds great, right? It might be great for a few people at the top, but so many get conned into buying the starter kit, paying for training, and then in turn make pennies. Run the other direction.

1) This is not a business. You are a distributor—paid on commission.

2) Nothing worth gaining in life is "easy." I liken this thought process to the get skinny with a pill mentality.

These companies range from skincare products (think Mary Kay and Arbonne) to jewelry (think Stella & Dot and Silpada) to household products (think Amway and Melaleuca). These networking marketing companies have gotten quite tricky. Many use the phrase "social selling," and some outright claim they are not a network marketing company—like Melaleuca. They will form companies with names like "Mom's Making Six Figures" and "Legacy Wealth Creation" to disguise that they are simply distributing some ele's products.

If you're not sure, search Wikipedia for a "list of network marketing companies" or www.BusinessForHome.com also has a fairly extensive list.

Another word of caution: be careful about getting sucked into the info-product/seminar world. The high you feel when you go to one of these events may lead you to buy into very expensive programming that you don't need. This group is also catering to the "get rich quick" market. I've seen people spend $100,000 on these programs, which is absurd! (Think Tony Robbins.) These coaches are trying to sell you their "lifestyle." But dig deep—is there content to their programs, or are they just putting neurolinguistic programming on steroids? It's easy to get sucked into the hype. After all, it feels good to be part of something and to be told that you ***can*** do it. Ask past participants if they have achieved the promises of the program. Dig deep to see what's behind the curtain.

There are no shortcuts to any place worth going.

– Beverly Sills

Keep Doubters At Bay

While you're probably feeling excitement about launching your dream business, please keep in mind that people may challenge your decision. Some may even call you crazy! (A word I welcome!) Most people are either personally fearful of such a decision or are straight-up jealous.

If you're married you may get push-back from your spouse. In some cases you may even find yourself drifting away from friends who continue to subscribe to the corporate ladder.

I have found the best antidote for these challenges is a good dose of confidence and a solid business plan, including sensible financial projections.

Imposter Syndrome

You will from time-to-time feel like a fraud. Note it, and get over it. Even some of the most successful women I've met tell me deep down that they are afraid of being "figured out." Even Tina Fey once confessed that she sometimes screams inside her head, "I'm a fraud! They're onto me!"

Dr. Valerie Young is a leading expert on the impostor syndrome, and author of award-winning book "The Secret Thoughts of Successful Women: Why Capable People Suffer from the Impostor Syndrome and How to Thrive in Spite of It." According to Dr. Young, boys are raised to bluff and exaggerate. Girls, on the other hand, learn early to distrust their opinions and stifle their voices. They discover they are judged by the highest physical, behavioral and intellectual standards. Perfection becomes the goal, and every flaw, mistake or criticism is internalized—slowly hollowing out self-confidence. Now you know why you shouldn't beat yourself up.

"I have written eleven books, but each time I think, 'uh oh, they're going to find out now. I've run a game on everybody, and they're going to find me out.' "

– Maya Angelou

Work/Life Integration

I am often asked—how do you balance work and life? My answer is quite simple "I don't"—my work is so much a part of my life that I couldn't possibly consider it to be something separate; an individual entity completely segregated from my personal life. My work does not feel like work.

I'm so passionate about my business because of the amazing women I get to support on a daily basis, through our space and strong community. I love helping others find what really lights them up... what allows them also to have work/life integration.

That's why I have an insatiable energy and don't feel drained after working 12 hour days. I don't mind having an inbox that is jam packed with requests, questions, and introductions because it is all a part of something so much bigger; something that I love, Hera Hub.

Make it a goal to thread your personal and professional life together. Incorporate things you enjoy into your business, so it feels like you're passing the time doing something pleasant rather than a task to be checked off of your list. Try to infuse "focused fun" by pinpointing what you love: drawing, talking, laughing, interesting conversation, list making, etc. and weave it into your business and work.

"Choose a job you love, and you will never have to work a day in your life."

– Confucius

Find Support

If you haven't done so already, it's time to find your tribe! If you don't have a Hera Hub close to you (and you are not in a position to open one yourself), here are a few non-virtual organizations I recommend.

Check our website - www.herahub.com/organizations - for an updated list.

Some of these are general, and some are industry-specific:

American Business Women's Association (ABWA) – www.abwa.org
Association for Women in Science (AWIS) – www.awis.org
Commercial Real Estate Women (CREW) – www.crewnetwork.org
Ellevate – www.ellevatenetwork.com
eWomen Network – www.ewomannetwork.com
Femfessionals – www.femfessionals.com
Healthcare Businesswomen's Association – www.hbanet.org
National Association for Female Executives – www.nafe.com
National Association of Professional Women (NAPW) – www.napw.com
National Association of Women Business Owners (NAWBO) – www.nawbo.org
National Association of Women MBAs (NAWMBA) – www.nawmba.org
Savor the Success – www.savorthesuccess.com
Society of Women Engineers – www.societyofwomenengineers.swe.org
Women 2.0 – www.women2.com
Women in Technology International (WITI) – www.witi.com

There are certainly many others out there—some regional, some local, some broadly focused on "professional" women. In general, this is focused on national professional women's organizations that have a focus on entrepreneurship and/or independent work (freelance/consultants).

If none of these are a fit and/or they are not in your area, then search www.meetup.com for "female entrepreneur."

If You Can't Find It, Build It

Finally, if nothing exists—which I can't imagine, unless you live in a town of 500 people—then start your own group! Meetup.com is a great way to pull people together and organize your group!

If you are interested in exploring what it would take to build a Hera Hub community in your town, check out www.HeraHubExpansion.com.

Why Passion Without Structure Can Lead to Failure

While being passionate about your venture will get you through the tough times, there is no substitute for building a solid foundation and structure for your business. I meet many female entrepreneurs who have spent thousands on educational programs, including health coaching, life coaching, business coaching and the like but won't invest in building the foundation of their business through a well thought-out business plan and logical financial projections. If you are going to take the time to invest in education be sure you save some money and energy to map out core business principles such as: target market, unique selling proposition, competitive advantage, revenue streams, etc.While we will go over some of this in the final section of the book, I have additional online resources available at www.StepsToStartup.com.

Don't get so carried away by passion that you fail to build a solid, practical foundation!

Find Your Muse

I have been incredibly grateful for many amazing women in my life, including my mother (the most amazing work ethic I've ever seen) and Linda Lattimore, my favorite mentor.

But above all, my muse, my inspiration, my soulmate, was my Grandma Hanson. Her positivity was contagious and her humor infectious. She had a heart of gold. She was a lover—always giving, sharing, and caring.

Astrid Pearson was born in Swedeburg, Nebraska. Her mother, Tekla Pearson, emigrated from Sweden in 1905. When my grandmother was 16, her family moved to Kingsburg, California (a small Swedish community in the Central Valley). She married my grandfather, John Hanson, at age 19. After he came back from WWII, they settled in Fresno, California and had a girl and two boys. My father, Don Hanson, was the middle child.

Grandma worked in an office in her early career but spent most of her life dedicated to taking care of family. It was the "Leave it to Beaver" era, and she was on board—building a beautiful life in their modest home, complete with ironing sheets and making sure there were plenty of warm cookies. She was a quintessential woman of the '50s, but underneath that perfectly embroidered apron, she had a feisty streak. She always knew what to say in a witty way.

While I wasn't the first of her ten grandchildren (my cousin Greg was born nine months before me), I was her first granddaughter. This was a very special bond. I remember spending summers in Fresno, just the two of us going out for glazed donut holes and then coming back and working in the garden. She had the most beautiful roses. She would always walk around barefoot and almost always wore slacks.

My Grandmother Taught Me …

- Why walking every day is the key to a long life
- How to love unconditionally
- The importance of family
- How to be graceful
- Why diplomacy is an art
- How to be feisty and sweet at the same time
- Why we must honor and respect our veterans
- How to truly take care of someone
- Why having an exceptional attitude is the number one determinant to a happy life

My grandfather passed away from a heart attack in 1987. My grandmother continued to live alone, never dated or even considered getting remarried. In her words, "Why would I want to take care of an old man?!"

Though you wouldn't know it by looking at her, my grandmother had no sight in her right eye from birth. Because of this, she never drove a car. This was another bonding experience that connected us later in life. Twelve years after my car accident, I picked up a 50-lb. bag of cement and tore my left retina. The repair was relatively successful but left me with significant scar tissue on the front of the eye.

Funny enough, we both ended up having cataract surgery in the same month—her cataracts due to old age and mine due to scar tissue after the surgery. Despite the surgery and a half-dozen direct steroid shots (yes, I can say anything is better than sticking a needle in your eye), I only regained partial sight. We used to always joke that between the two of us we made a perfect pair of eyes!

Breaking The Mold

At age 88, she decided to move from her mild Protestant church to an all-black Baptist church. This was partially because it was within walking distance (about a mile) and partially because she loved music. I remember accompanying her one Sunday. It was so much fun to see everyone dote over this little white-haired old lady who always sat in the back pew. She had found a wonderful family in that church.

She outlived my grandfather by 25 years. She continued to walk every day and volunteer at the veteran's hospital two days a week. When she couldn't take the bus anymore, she got a ride.

She never took much more than an aspirin up until the point when she had to be removed from her home and moved into assisted living in 2009. Sadly, she began to weaken (several infections set in) and passed away in her sleep in October 2012.

The memory of her still inspires me every day to build a supportive community where women can inspire one another.

And... one final nod to another amazing woman in my life... my namesake, Felena Hendrickson. No, I wasn't named after the main character in a 1950s Marty Robbins song "Felena, the wicked maiden from El Paso, Texas." I was named after my great-grandmother, who was born in Sweden in 1900. She immigrated to the United States in her early twenties. I'm proud of my heritage - half Swedish, quarter Danish, and quarter Norwegian. And I'm blessed to have both amazing female and male role models in my life!

Please go find what inspires you and etch it in your mind so you too can take flight!

Now It's Your Turn!

It's time to spread your wings and let all of your passions, strengths, talents and vision come together to launch your dream business. The final section of this book will give you the foundational tools that are needed. You're in good hands!

Part 4
Taking Flight

Chapter 11
Steps to Startup

I HOPE THAT BY this point you have a good idea of what your dream business looks like. When you're ready, this next section of the book will guide you through seventeen steps that will help you build a strong foundation for your business.

While I've outlined the steps here, I HIGHLY recommend that you go to **www.StepsToStartup.com** and sign up for online access to this content-rich platform. This will allow you to view video tutorials and access all the web links for each step.

Want access for free? All you have to do register at www.StepsToStartup.com. In order to prove that you purchased this book you must take a picture of yourself holding the book (get out your selfie stick!) You will then need to post this picture on our Facebook page - www.Facebook.com/FlightClubBook or on Twitter by tagging @FelenaHanson. You will be asked to paste the link to your post when registering. While Facebook makes this easy, on Twitter it's not as obvious. We will have directions on how to grab this link on the registration page.

I created StepsToStartup, not because of a lack of information, but rather because of the overload of information available online. I find that many people are simply overwhelmed by all the moving parts in setting up a business correctly—where to register, how to set up systems, what systems to use, etc.

The steps are broken down into five major categories:

- Big Picture
- Registration
- Marketing
- Operations
- Financing

Let's get started!

This information is only related to set-up of U.S. based companies.

BIG PICTURE

1. Customer Discovery

Before you do anything, you *must* determine that you're offering the right product or service to the right customer. Identify what your customer needs. This will give you the confidence that you're going in the right direction.

If you can't find customers willing to talk about their problems, you won't be able to find customers.

Connect with at least ten people who happen to be your target customers and ask them to give you twenty minutes of their time. Offer to buy them lunch. These conversations will help you formalize the need and how your business can *solve it*!

Here are some suggested questions for your brief interview. These are only a starting point, so feel free to add your own.

- What is your biggest frustration with ____________?
- Can you tell me about the last time that happened? (Try to get them to tell you a story.)
- What, if anything, have you done to solve that challenge?
- Why did you make that decision? (Customers don't buy the what, they buy the why. You can use this answer to help craft your marketing copy.)
- What didn't you like about the solutions you've tried?
- How much money have you spent to solve the challenge?
- How much time and money are you still willing to invest (if the problem wasn't solved)?

One important note: if they aren't looking for solutions already, then you must ask yourself, "Is this a big enough problem?" For someone to make a bet on you—a startup, an unknown entity—you must offer to solve a problem so pressing that customers are actively searching for solutions.

Always remember to follow up with a thank-you note. Think about adding a Starbucks gift card in there, too. After all, these people might end up actually being your customers.

2. Simple Business Canvas

According to conventional wisdom, the first thing every founder must do is create a business plan—a static document that describes the size of the opportunity, the problem to be solved, and the solution that the new venture will provide. Typically, it includes a five-year forecast for income, profits, and cash flow. A business plan is essentially a research exercise, written in isolation at a desk before an entrepreneur has even begun to build a product. The assumption is that it's possible to figure out most of the unknowns about your business in advance, before you actually execute the idea. It is important to keep in mind that the business plan is a work in progress, and it can be adjusted if need be. Thus, we advocate for a simple one- or two-page document—the Business Model Canvas—that outlines the main areas of your business.

The Business Model Canvas was initially proposed by Alexander Osterwalder, based on his earlier work on Business Model Ontology. Since the release of Osterwalder's work in 2008, new canvases (such as the Lean Canvas by Ash Maurya) for specific niches have appeared.

In addition to finding the Lean Canvas template on StepsToStartup.com you should also download our financial projections template to ensure you're able to make your business model work.

3. Naming

You want a name that will describe your business and be memorable to your target market, but it must (obviously) be unique to your company. What if there is another company in the US that is already using the name you want? Say there is a business in Oregon with the same name you want to use, and both of you only do business locally; using the same name may not pose an issue (for example, A+ Tutoring San Diego and A+ Tutoring Portland). It is unlikely that consumers would get confused and accidentally hire the other business when they meant to hire you.

However, if you plan to expand and do business in other states (or even nationally or internationally), you don't want any confusion. Keep the future of your business in mind as you choose your name. Also keep in mind that if another company has the name you want to use, it may own the rights to the website address (URL) that corresponds to that name, and thus may cause confusion, especially if you're an "info-preneur" (offering knowledge online).

Run each potential name through the following steps:

1. Do a simple Google search of the name without quotation marks.
2. Do a simple Google search of the name with quotation marks—this narrows the search.
3. Check for the domain availability using a site like bluehost.com.
    a. If the domain you want is taken, find out who owns it on whois.net.
    b. Are they actively using the site or just sitting on it? If they're sitting on it, is it for sale? (We don't necessarily recommend buying domains from someone, but if you find you must, make sure you negotiate!) If the domain is available, make sure to purchase it. You can do this through sites such as GoDaddy or BlueHost.
    c. Can you abbreviate the URL without confusing your potential customers? For example, if www.InnovativeBodyScience.com is not available, would you try www.IBS.com? Think about what else that acronym is used for. Could you use www.InnovativeBody.com? Probably not too bad. We do rec-

ommend staying away from abbreviations—going from www.PerspectiveMarketing.com to www.PerspectiveMktg.com can be a pain in the long run. Think about how many times you will be saying your domain name out loud.

4. Check USPTO.gov to make sure no one has the trademark in your classification.
5. If all signs are positive, then take a week or so to do a market test with friends and family on the name. What do they think of when they hear the name? What type of business do they think it is, based on the name alone?
6. How will your name work visually? Think of your logo, marketing materials, etc. (we'll get into more details in the branding section).

Go to StepsToStartup.com for more information on naming.

Do You Need A Tagline?

A tagline is optional. We recommend considering a tagline if your business name does not describe what you do. For example, because Hera Hub is not descriptive, our tagline is "Workspace for Women," which simply describes what we do. For more information, check out the great article on the StepsToStartup platform titled: How to Write a Good Tagline.

Protecting Your Business Name

If you are planning to operate only in your local area, you may not want to go to the trouble and expense of filing a state or federal trademark for your business.

Local Protection

According to common law, the business that uses a particular trade name first has the legal right to that name. Common-law protection does not require specific filings with the government. Therefore, this type of protection may be sufficient if you just plan to do business locally.

If you decide to file for either state or federal trademarks, we recommend hiring an attorney.

State Protection

- ***Register Your Legal Business Name.*** To extend the protection that a common-law registration provides, register your legal name with your state. The legal name of your LLC or corporation is already registered with your state government if you have incorporated your business. However, if you own a sole proprietorship or a partnership, contact your secretary of state to register. **There will be more about this in the next section.**
- ***File a DBA or Fictitious Name.*** If you are doing business under a name that is different from your legal business name, you will need to file a DBA, otherwise known as a "doing business as" name or a fictitious name. You are using a fictitious name when you advertise your business under another name or if your business is widely known by the public under another name. **There will be more about this in the next section.**
- ***Register for a State Trademark.*** Filing a state trademark for your business name, trade name, or domain name does not require as much time and money as a federal trademark. A state trademark also provides protection in states like Alabama that do not require businesses to file trade names with the state government. If you are planning to do business solely in your state, a state trademark will provide you with the necessary protection. *Learn about how to file a trademark with your state at StepsToStarup.com.*

National Protection

- ***Register for a Federal Trademark.*** If you are doing business across states or plan to launch your business nationally, you will want to trademark your trade name with the federal government. By registering your trade name with the US Patent and Trademark Office, you can protect your trade name against infringement. For a trademark registration to remain valid, a "Declaration of Use" must be filed (1) between the fifth and sixth year following registration and (2) within the year before the end of every ten-year period after the date of registration.

When registering a mark, it is important to file the application in the proper class. If you seek to register a mark in the wrong class, your application will be cancelled, and your fee will not be refunded, so getting the classification right during the application process saves time and money. Review the classes that may be appropriate. Each class's web page contains an extensive list of potential goods or services for that class. There are forty-five classes in all: thirty-four for products and eleven for services.

DISCLAIMER: While this can be done on your own, we recommend hiring an attorney to make sure your information is submitted correctly and in the correct categories. Application for registration, per class, ranges from $275–$375 (depending on if you're filing online or via a paper form). An attorney will charge you an additional fee for services on top of the filing fee. This may be well worth the investment.

REGISTRATION

4. Licensing & Permits

Again, we will focus on pointing you back to the StepsTo-Startup website for this section, as much of what you'll need to complete is through state and federal websites.

As always, we suggest you consult a local attorney to ensure you're complying with all local, state, and federal agencies.

This section covers:

1. Local—city/county
2. State
3. Federal

5. Banking & Credit Cards

Once you have your business name (fictitious or otherwise,) you must set up a separate bank account. It is imperative to keep everything separate for ease of tracking expenditures and revenue!

I can't emphasize this enough. I see so many businesses commingle personal and business funds. This is not only an accounting headache it's also a personal liability issue. You are piercing the corporate veil if you co-mingle. Talk to your CPA or attorney - they will give you a sufficient scare on this.

Similarly, if you're going to use credit, you must also get a separate credit card for your business (ask your bank for this when setting up your account.) It doesn't have to be a business credit card, just a card that you *only* use for business. Contact your bank to see what paperwork they need from you in order to open an account or credit card under your business name.

An organized system for tracking your business finances is crucial. Set yourself up for success by developing a system from the get-go.

Accepting Credit Cards

Some business owners balk at the 3% processing fees, but running after clients who won't pay will cost you a lot more than 3%.

If you're a product-based company, you ***must*** *accept credit cards.* If you're a service-based company, you can wait on this and see how it goes. We actually recommend getting a credit card number from a client for all your contracts as a backup plan. Write into your contract that if the bill is more than ___ days late you will automatically charge the customer's card. You can also include an additional late fee of 3% if you choose.

Credit Card Options

Start with your bank. Ask them questions about the best solutions for you and your business. You may be able to get by with a very simple payment system, or you might need something with more capabilities (e.g., linking to inventory, multiple store locations, etc.). Think through your needs and make sure the system you choose can keep up with the amount of business you do and makes it easy to do business.

There are also alternative options worth exploring, such as PayPal, Square, and Stripe.

6. Record Keeping

Set up your accounting and record-keeping system and learn about the taxes your new company is responsible for paying (we'll cover this more later). Generally, you are required to keep company documents for three years. These documents include a list of all owners and addresses, as well as copies of all formation documents, financial statements, annual reports, and amendments or changes to the company. All tax and corporate filings should be kept for at least three years.

Create a filing system—digital or hard copy—that will keep your records organized and accessible. Think about the types of files you'll be keeping—contracts, expenses, formation documents, etc.—and set up your system accordingly. When tracking your expenses, make sure you have a system for categorizing each expense and that you use the system consistently. This will be important for deducting expenses on taxes, which we will cover in the tax section.

Recommended Platforms

The two main small-business bookkeeping software tools are QuickBooks and FreshBooks. QuickBooks has been around a lot longer, and it is seen as a much more serious accounting platform. The desktop version is nice if you don't have Internet access and would rather pay one cost up front, although it won't keep itself updated like the cloud-based software.

FreshBooks is quite a bit more "hip," and it can definitely get the job done for freelancers with straightforward businesses that are based on services or billable time.

We recommend that you hire or work with an accountant to set up and manage your books. Having a knowledgeable person on your team will save a lot of time and prevent things from going wrong, which can be expensive and cause many unnecessary headaches.

Much more information can be found at StepsToStartup.com.

Deducting Business Expenses

Deducting business expenses is extremely important. The more legitimate deductions you can take, the less taxable income you will have. This means higher profits, and who doesn't want that? Several types of expenses can be deducted, many of which are often overlooked. The IRS has some helpful information, along with Entrepreneur.com. Be aware of the types of items you can deduct, and make sure you track those expenditures. Remember to be consistent with how you categorize your spending, and have an organized filing system in which to keep receipts/invoices, etc.

If you are self-employed or starting a small business, you have to pay double the Social Security tax because federal law requires that the employer pay half and the employee pay half—you are both.

Easily Overlooked Business Expenses

Here are some additional routine deductions that many business owners miss (courtesy of Nolo):

- audio and videotapes related to business skills
- bank service charges
- business association dues
- business gifts
- business-related magazines and books
- casual labor and tips
- casualty and theft losses
- coffee and beverage service
- commissions
- consultant fees
- online computer services related to business
- parking and meters
- postage
- promotion and publicity
- seminars and trade shows
- taxi and bus fare
- telephone calls away from the business

Note: Just because you didn't get a receipt doesn't mean you can't deduct the expense, so keep track of those small items.

7. Entity Setup

Business Structure

There are many options regarding the legal entity of your business, but you must pick a structure under which to operate.

Before you start operating your business, you will want to create an entity that works as your business operator. There are several forms of business structures for you to consider. Selecting the business entity that is right for you will involve tax, business, and estate planning, along with financial considerations. In this section, we discuss the various structures and identify the advantages and disadvantages of each. The legal structure you choose will determine the organization, debt liability, and tax requirements, as well as other aspects of business questions.

The quick chart below shows your entity options. Much more information can be found on the StepsToStartup platform.

Sole Proprietorship	Partnership	Corporations
• Independently owned by one person • Unincorporated • Considered an extension of the owner rather than a separate legal entity	• Owned by two or more people • General Partnership: each partner is held personally liable for all debts, taxes, and other claims • Limited Partnership: one partner is limited in personal liability	• Three types: LLCs and subchapter S and C corporations • Must complete incorporation process • Legal entity that is separate from the people who own, manage, and control it

8. Tax Setup

Every business entity is responsible for federal and state income taxes. If your business is a sole proprietorship, partnership, S corporation, or limited liability company (LLC), pretax income is reported on your individual tax return. If your business is a regular corporation, it will be subject to corporate income taxes. Different reporting forms are required for different types of organizations. In some cases, an Employment Identification Number (EIN) is required for tax reporting.

Federal Taxes

Every business must file federal taxes. Below are the key components to be aware of when setting up your taxes and figuring out which taxes apply to your business.

Estimated Taxes—*This is one of the areas new business owners most often miss!*

As an employee, you had the convenience of having your employer withhold and remit taxes throughout the year, but as a business owner, you are responsible for sending quarterly estimated tax payments. These are due on April 15, June 15, September 15, and January 15 of every year. The January date is for the preceding tax year. If any of these dates fall on a holiday or weekend, the payments are typically due the following business day. A best practice is to put these dates into your calendar, setting a reminder several weeks before the due date.

How do you calculate the estimated tax payment amount?

Because you don't know in advance your tax liability for the upcoming year, most business owners calculate the minimum needed to avoid incurring a penalty.

If you expect your earnings this year to be comparable to last year's, use last year's tax return for your starting estimate. Divide last year's total tax by four to reach the minimum estimated quarterly tax payment. Avoid penalties by paying at least 90% of the taxes you owe for this year—or as much as the prior year's tax liability.

If you anticipate that your financial situation is likely to vary from last year's, then make your best estimate early on. Conduct a midyear tax review to make adjustments.

Sole proprietorships, partnerships, S corporations, and most

LLCs should see Form 1040-ES for estimation worksheets. Corporations should see Form 1120-W.

How do you remit and budget for estimated tax payments?

If you fail to pay your quarterly estimated taxes, you can incur IRS penalties, which vary each year. Review Form 1040-ES and mail your payments using the vouchers included. Once your business is in the system, you should start receiving vouchers from the IRS at the end of each year. You can also submit payments online through the Electronic Federal Tax Payment System.

WE STRONGLY RECOMMEND CONSULTING A CPA ABOUT PAYING QUARTERLY ESTIMATED TAXES.

Self-Employment Taxes

Self-employment tax is a tax consisting of Social Security and Medicare taxes, and is primarily for individuals who work for themselves. It is similar to the Social Security and Medicare taxes withheld from the pay of most wage earners.

You figure self-employment tax (SE tax) yourself using Schedule SE (Form 1040). You can deduct the employer-equivalent portion of your SE tax in figuring your adjusted gross income (which wage earners cannot).

See StepsToStartup.com for the most up-to-date information on fees.

Reporting Payments to Independent Contractors

If you pay independent contractors, you will have to file Form 1099-MISC (Miscellaneous Income) to report payments for services performed for your trade or business.

Employment Taxes for Small Businesses

If you have employees, you are responsible for several federal, state, and local taxes. As an employer, you must withhold federal income tax withholding, Social Security, and Medicare taxes, as well as Federal Unemployment Tax Act (FUTA) taxes.

**If you have employees set aside some extra money for FUTA taxes. If your state runs into issues they will bill you back. This can cost hundreds of dollars per employee and will come without warning. One of the joys of being a small business owner!*

We recommend using a payroll service, both for contractors and employees. This will help streamline all of the steps associated with paying your employees.

MARKETING

9. Pricing

A lot goes into deciding how to price your services or products. You likely want a price that keeps you competitive, but if you price too low, your potential customers may perceive that your product or service is less valuable, and if you price too high, you may lose customers. Some basic formulas can help you set a price and make sure you are covering your material costs and your time.

Create a One-Page Price List

We don't mean that you need to create a strict price sheet that you will live and die by—just have an idea of the price you want to charge for your various goods and/or services. You need to know how much it costs you to produce your goods or service and how much your own time and expertise is worth. That way, when someone approaches you about an order, job, etc., you can offer at least a ballpark estimate of what you might charge them.

10. Branding

Develop a Business Identity

What does your business say? What do you want it to represent? Here, you will be creating your business identity—your brand. The "brand" of your business is essentially the take-home message from your marketing—for example, Volvo is equated with safety and Swiss watches are known for their fine craftsmanship.

What is *your* brand about? Are you the low-price leader in your field? Are you the greenest, fastest, or most experienced? Your marketing and design should all form a cohesive message that revolves around that key concept.

Create a Logo and Business Cards

A professionally created logo can make your business look professional and established. Conversely, a bad logo will reflect poorly on your business. Unless you are a graphic designer or logo expert, we recommend engaging with a professional graphic designer to develop your logo and design your business cards.

Company Identity/Logo Design Questionnaire

You should ask yourself a few questions when you're thinking about what you want your logo to look and feel like. Keep in mind that you want your logo to speak to the same brand message you've already created, so if your brand is about being simple and streamlined, don't get too wild with your logo.

Requirements

Is there anything that your logo is required to have or not have? Legal disclosures? A very specific color? A limit to the number of colors? A certain size? Pictures or text? Try not to limit yourself too much with this, but include what is needed.

Style

What "style" are you aiming for? Use words and phrases like "cutting edge," "modern," "old-fashioned," "fun," "high-tech," "warm and fuzzy," "curvy," "straight-lined," "cartooned," "conservative," "professional," etc. Find examples of these styles from any industry and figure out what you like and dislike. This is the best way to communicate the "feel" you want.

Contrast

Do you like a design with bright color contrasts, or do you prefer a more subdued logo? Bright colors make your logo stand out and are often more memorable. More subdued color schemes tend to appear more traditional (and arguably more professional) and are more easily reproduced as faxes and copies, since they don't rely on color reproduction.

Colors

What colors do you want to use? What colors do you love or hate?

Text

Is there text that must be incorporated into your logo? If you have a tagline (or any other text) that you want included in the design, think about how to incorporate it.

Composition

Do you want a graphical element to your logo, or do you prefer stylized text? (For example, IBM and Microsoft logos are stylized text. AT&T and Apple Computers use graphical elements.)

Graphics

If you prefer a graphical component (sometimes called an icon), do you want a nonsymbolic shape, or do you want a picture of something? (Nike's "swoosh" is a nonsymbolic shape. Apple's "apple" is obviously symbolic of an apple.)

Fonts

What type of font do you prefer—serif (e.g., Times New Roman and Courier) or sans serif (e.g., Arial and Tahoma)? (It's okay not to have a preference here.) If you need ideas, check out fonts.com.

Examples

Finally, find logos you like *and* dislike, and figure out *why*. If you don't know where to find a bunch of logos, try a Google image search. Go to Google Images and search for "logo" or, for a more specific search, search for "logo" and words related to your industry. This could give you inspiration for your own logo.

11. Marketing Tactics

Rule #1 of marketing is <u>know your target market</u>! Focus on the things that will actually reach those people. Figuring out exactly what strategies to use and how to execute your marketing with various platforms can be tricky.

Seek support from the Hera Hub community or take advantage of the workshops through <u>Hera LABS</u>.

Base your marketing strategy on what will actually reach your customers.

Ask yourself these questions:

- Who exactly is my target customer?
- What do they read, watch, and listen to?
- What is their trigger point—the point at which they know they need my product or service?
- Who is in the life of my customer at this time?
- How can I build a strong referral network?

<u>Word of Caution</u>: You likely won't need to have a profile or presence on every social media website out there. Find one or two that your customers engage with, and make sure you have a strong presence there. There may also be other ways to reach them where they will be more receptive.

Choose the top ten marketing tactics you will use:

- Advertising Specialties
- Affiliate Marketing
- Articles
- Audio Marketing
- Auto-responders
- Automobile Signage
- Award Recognition
- Banner Ads
- Billboards
- Blogging
- Bonus Offers
- Brochures
- Business Cards
- Case Studies

- Catalogs
- Cause Marketing
- Community Events
- Contests
- Craigslist
- Cross-promotion
- Customer Loyalty Programs
- Direct Mail
- Door Hangers
- Email Marketing
- Endorsements
- Ezines
- Facebook
- Feedback forms
- Flyers
- Gift Cards
- Google+
- Google Helpouts
- Guest Blogging
- Infomercials
- Link Strategies
- LinkedIn
- LinkedIn Group Discussions
- Magazine Advertising
- Media outreach
- Mobile Ads
- Newsletters (e-mail & snail mail)
- Newspaper advertising
- Pay-per-click
- Pinterest
- Podcasting
- Pop-ups
- Postcards
- Posters
- Sales Presentations
- Public Relations
- Press Kits
- Radio Advertising
- Raffles
- Referral Marketing
- Reviews (Customer and Professional)
- Rewards Programs
- Sales Calls
- Sales Letters
- Search Engine Optimization
- Seminars
- Signature Files
- Sign Spinners
- SlideShare

- Speaking Engagements
- Special Events
- Special-occasion Gifts
- Strategic Alliances
- Surveys
- Sweepstakes
- Telemarketing
- Tele-seminars
- Television Advertising
- Testimonials
- Thank-you Pages
- Trade Journal Ads
- Twitter
- Training
- Tutorials
- Tumblr
- Videos
- Viral Marketing
- White Papers
- Webinars
- Word of Mouth
- Workshops
- YouTube.com

12. Online Presence

Yes, ideally, you need a website. However, if you're a solo service provider like a marketing consultant, CPA, or attorney, you can probably get away with a well-done LinkedIn profile for a few months until you get everything else in order.

This is my number one piece of advice: website or not, you *must* have a killer LinkedIn profile.

If you're ready to dive in, there are several ways to set up and build a website. The most popular options are WordPress and Squarespace.

There are pros and cons to each option. For comparisons, check the StepsToStartup site

Hosting: If you go with WordPress, you will need a separate hosting company.

Register a Domain Name and Purchase Hosting Services

Get a domain name that matches your business name—you should have checked on the available domain in the naming step earlier. We still prefer ".com" to any other extension: it seems more official and professional.

Set up email with your firstname@domain.com. You can route this through Gmail or other platforms, but it looks more professional to use the domain account instead of just having the @gmail extension. A Yahoo or Gmail address (or a website with free hosting and a name like mysite.wordpress.com) makes it seem like either (a) you are not running a real business or (b) you don't plan to be around long.

Tip: For SEO purposes, it's recommended that you purchase your domain for ten years.

Set Up Social Media Profiles

Getting set up on the major social media channels (Facebook, LinkedIn, and Twitter, to start) will make it easier to use them for marketing later. Also, it's important to reserve your brand as a profile name. You may want to get set up on Facebook, Twitter, Instagram, Google+, and create a LinkedIn Company Page; however, you might not need a strong presence on every social media channel.

Thinking back to the marketing section, put your efforts toward the sites that your target customers actually use. Make sure those profiles are polished and professional. Also, think beyond the usual sites. Consider social sites that are important to your industry. Are there more specialized social websites that could help you reach your audience?

Professional Mailing Address

You will need a professional mailing address for your business. For many reasons, including safety and professionalism, it is important that you *not* list your home address on your public business documents (website, business cards, etc.). You may register your business to your home address, but be careful about what's getting linked: once a website like Google grabs on to your home address, it can be challenging to update.

The reason we have this step listed in the "Online Presence" section is because you will need to link your professional mailing address to review sites (such as Google Local and Yelp) and your e-mail marketing campaigns. Spam laws require you to list a real physical address, not a PO box.

You can get a physical address at a place like a UPS Store or Mail Boxes Etc., but when someone Googles your address, the street view will show—you guessed it—a UPS Store or Mail Boxes Etc.

The best solution is to get mail service through your local coworking space or executive suite.

OPERATIONS

13. Contracts

It is important to have well-crafted contracts that are appropriate for their intended use.

A business contract is often used for:

- Hiring or being employed as an independent contractor
- Leases and real estate
- Partnerships and joint ventures
- Confidentiality agreements
- Noncompete agreements
- Client agreements

You can save money by drafting your own agreement based on online research and taking your draft to an attorney to polish (instead of having the attorney draft it from scratch), but **never implement a contract without first having an attorney review it!**

A good place to get templates is Entrepreneur.com.

14. Insurance

There are many types of insurance for businesses, but they are usually packaged as "General Business Insurance" or a "Business Owner's Policy." This can cover everything from product liability to company vehicles. A decent policy can run as little as $300 per year and offer a great extra level of protection. Below is a list of common types of insurance you may want to consider:

- Business Owner's Policy
- General Liability Insurance
- Product Liability Insurance
- Professional Liability Insurance
- Property Insurance
- Home-based Business Insurance

- Commercial Auto Insurance
- Worker's Compensation
- Data Breach
- Business Interruption Insurance
- Errors and Omissions Insurance

Workers' compensation insurance is required for businesses of any size, *even if you only have one employee.* A policy can be purchased directly from the state of California. Insurance varies by state, so make sure to check that you meet your state's requirements. For FAQs about workers' compensation see StepsToStartup.com

Other types of insurance products are available that may be specific to the nature of your operations, including cyber liability insurance, inland marine (specialty equipment) insurance, EPLI (Employment Practices Liability Insurance), and more. Your agent or broker will be able to explain the coverage options and determine which products are best suited to your needs and exposure.

A Commercial Package Policy (CPP) offers a way to package multiple lines of business insurance. This can eliminate redundancy, provide flexibility, and leave fewer gaps in coverage. The primary benefit is that you can put multiple lines of insurance under one policy, thus making administration much simpler. This structure has the potential to reduce costs, so be sure to inquire about this policy structure when setting up your insurance. Worker's compensation is separate from the CPP.

Health Insurance

If you're self-employed (as a freelancer, consultant, independent contractor), you can use the individual Health Insurance Marketplace.

If your business has even one employee (other than yourself, a spouse, a family member, or an owner), you may be able to use the SHOP Marketplace for small businesses to obtain coverage for yourself and your employees. See the article on StepsToStartup.com titled: "How do I know if I'm self-employed or a small employer?" to learn more.

Coverage options for the self-employed:

- When you fill out a Marketplace application, you'll find out if you qualify for premium tax credits and other savings on a health plan. This will be based on your income and household size.
- You'll also find out if you qualify for free or low-cost coverage through the Medicaid and CHIP programs in your state. This will depend on your income, household size, and other factors.
- Do a quick check to see if your expected income is in the range to save.

In the Marketplace, you can choose among several categories of coverage, from plans with low premiums that mainly protect you in worst-case scenarios to plans where you'll pay more each month but less out of pocket when you get health care services.

Self-employment Income and Marketplace Savings

When you fill out a Health Insurance Marketplace application, you'll have to estimate your net self-employment income. Marketplace savings are based on your **estimated net income for the year you're getting coverage, not last year's income.**

When you're self-employed, it can be hard to estimate your income for the coming months or year. Check with your CPA on this.

Most Americans must have minimum essential coverage. If you don't, you'll pay a penalty. This is true no matter what your job status is.

15. Team

You may not be ready to hire your first employee, but that doesn't mean you shouldn't start thinking about building your team.

Your team should be made up of your go-to advisers, such as an attorney, CPA, marketing consultant, bookkeeper/accountant, etc. This team will help you troubleshoot, answer questions, serve as a sounding board, or maybe just act as support staff. Many of these trusted advisers can be found within local business organizations. The most important point is: *don't do it alone*!

What should you outsource?

Start by keeping a list of tasks you don't enjoy in your business (the ones you find yourself procrastinating around). These are the first things you'll need to explore outsourcing. For example, if you hate accounting, then find a good bookkeeper.

Again, more helpful information about team building and working with interns can be found at StepsToStartup.com

16. Systems & Organization

There are several things to consider when thinking of how best to incorporate and use technology to your advantage. Consider every aspect of your business and what technology is best suited to each task. Think of all your daily operations and what it would take to complete them.

Prepare the business as if someone needed to take it over and run it for you. This means having methods in place to process orders, pay bills, pay employees, pay taxes, maintain your permits, keep records, etc. Basically, try to make the operational aspect of the business as automated and efficient as possible so you can concentrate on growing your business. If more than one person will be working with you, it could be helpful to create an operations manual. Technology will help you in systemizing your business!

Phone/Voicemail System

Will you deal with a high volume of calls? How many phone lines will you need to conduct business efficiently? Can you get away with just using your cell phone? Often, the answer is yes. Several options can assist with handling phone calls and voicemails, including:

- Phone.com
- Grasshopper.com
- CallRuby.com
- Line2.com—allows you to route your personal and business line through your cell phone.

Scheduling Software

It is imperative that you have a good way to schedule meetings and appointments. Stay on top of your schedule and make it easy to handle everything you have going on. We recommend programs such as:

- Scheduleonce.com—our personal favorite. Integrates well with Gmail and is highly customizable.
- Acuity—excellent choice for a business model that schedules successive appointments.
- TimeTrade—good for a business that schedules lots of meetings.
- Schedulista—integrates with many online platforms using a .csv file.

E-mail Marketing Programs

Once you've started to build your database, an e-mail marketing platform is a critical part of marketing communications. When sending out an e-mail newsletter or any kind of promotion, you *must* include a physical address and an option to opt out.

Some of the most popular e-mail marketing programs include:

- MailChimp
- Constant Contact
- FuseMail
- Rackspace
- Emma

For more information about email marketing, check StepsTo-Startup.com.

Customer Relationship Management (CRM) System

You may want a hand in organizing and automating information related to sales, marketing, and customer service. This is where the CRM system comes in handy. Some CRM options include:

- Zoho
- OnePage CRM
- Pipedrive
- Salesforce

Other Software

Some platforms offer a range of services that meet many needs. Some services offer solutions for scheduling, bookkeeping, email, banking, and much more—all through one company. Some of these are:

- 17 Hats—for an all-in-one approach to almost everything your business needs. If you want to get a better idea of what 17 Hats actually does, go to StepsToStartup.com.
- Google Apps for Work
- Office 365 for Business
- Trello—a visual organization platform.

Accounting

As mentioned earlier, your accounting software is critical. Understanding your business needs and the capabilities of the software is important. We covered this earlier, but you can take another look at QuickBooks and FreshBooks.

FINANCING

17. Start-up Capital

When exploring your funding options, there are several factors to consider:

- Are your needs short-term or long-term?
- How quickly will you be able to pay back the loan or provide return on their investment?
- Is the money for operating expenses or for capital expenditures that will become assets, such as equipment or real estate?
- Do you need all the money now or in smaller amounts over several months?
- Are you willing to assume all the risk if your company doesn't succeed, or do you want someone to share the risk?

The answers to these questions will help you prioritize the many funding options available.

Fundamentally, there are two types of business financing:

- **Debt financing**—you borrow the money and agree to pay it back in a particular time frame at a set interest rate. You owe the money whether your venture succeeds or not. Bank loans are what most people typically think of as debt financing, but we will explore many other options below.
- **Equity financing**—you sell partial ownership of your company in exchange for cash. The investors assume all (or most) of the risk: if the company fails, they lose their money, but if it succeeds, they typically make a *much* greater return on their investment than conventional interest rates. In other words, equity financing is far more expensive if your company is successful, but far less expensive if it isn't.

Because investors take on a much higher risk than lenders, they are typically far more involved in your company. This can be a mixed blessing. They will likely offer advice and connections to help grow your business. However, if their plan is to exit your company in two to three years with a substantial return on their investment and your motivation is the long-term sustainable growth of the company, you may find yourself at odds with them as the company grows. Be careful not to give up too much control of your company.

Friends and Family

This is still your best source for both loans and equity deals. They are typically less stringent regarding your credit and their expected return on investment. One caveat: structure the deal with the same legal rigor you would with anyone else, or it may create problems down the road when you look for additional financing. Prepare a business plan and formal documents—you'll both feel better, and it's good practice for later.

Credit Cards

These are great tools for cash-flow management, assuming you use them just for that and not for long-term financing. Keep one or two cards with no balances and pay them off every month, giving yourself a thirty- to sixty-day float with no interest. Low introductory rates on some cards make them some of the cheapest money around. Managed well, they're extremely effective; managed poorly, they're extremely expensive.

Bank Loans

These come in all shapes and sizes, from microloans of a few hundred dollars (typically offered by local community banks) to six-figure loans from major national banks. These are much easier to obtain when backed by assets (home equity or an IRA) or third-party guarantors (e.g., government-sponsored SBA loans or a cosigner). If you obtain a line of credit rather than a fixed-amount loan, you don't start paying interest until you actually spend the money.

Leasing

This is the way to go if you need big-ticket items such as equipment, vehicles, or even computers. Your supplier will help you explore this.

Angel Investors

These people fill the gap between friends and family and venture capitalists, who now rarely even look at investments below $1 million. Enlist a savvy financial adviser to structure the deal. Consider AngelList, a website that brings together investors and startups.

Private Lending

This represents a viable alternative when the bank says "no." Private lenders look for the same information and will conduct similar due diligence as the banks, but they typically specialize in an industry and are more willing to take on higher-risk loans if they see the potential. Consider Dealstruck.

Supplier Credit to Meet Your Business Needs Quickly

A supplier credit is another financing option for your small-scale business. It is a preferred choice of small business owners, as the process allows them to meet their business needs more quickly. It is easy to obtain a supplier credit, where the supplier of your products will allow you to pay for the goods they deliver within a certain period, usually weeks or months. If you are a good debtor, supplier creditors will be happy to approve you for a larger credit line or extend your repayment terms to help you position your business more effectively while getting the needed products to increase your sales.

SBA Loans

A Small Business Administration loan is another funding option to consider. It does not provide the loan directly to you as the business owner, but merely provides a guarantee that you will pay your business loan to a creditor. An SBA loan can be a good backup source to help you obtain the loan you need to fund your business, regardless of its size.

Secured Working Capital Loan

You can use your business assets as collateral in order to apply for a secured working capital loan. With this kind of business financing option, you will be able to obtain a lower interest rate with more flexible repayment terms. You will be able to obtain cash in exchange for your assets, with the ability to redeem your assets upon full payment of your business loan. However, there is a danger of losing all your business assets: your creditor may seize them if you default on your financial obligations.

Crowdfunding

The advent and relative growth of crowdfunding platforms such as Kickstarter and Indiegogo have proven to be a great advancement for nonprofits and other organizations, but they also offer startup founders a unique opportunity to sell their ideas directly to the consuming public.

Switching From Employee To Entrepreneurial Mindset

1. **Dream and do at the same time.** *You must be the long-term visionary while simultaneously keeping the day-to-day tasks under control. As an entrepreneur, you have to project your mind forward, thinking about the potential pitfalls and opportunities that lie around the corner and making decisions based on uncertainty.*

2. **The buck stops with you.** *In a* **job**, *you're often waiting for things to happen—for someone to give you permission*

or for your boss to give you the "green light." Entrepreneurs have an incredible opportunity to create something from nothing, but this means you must be 100% self-motivated. **You** *decide what you do, how you do it, and when you do it. While many long for this kind of autonomy, the reality of all this decision making can be challenging for some.*

3. **Get comfortable with being uncomfortable.** *As an employee, you have a significant safety net. In most cases, you have coworkers to support you if you drop the ball or make a mistake. You typically have checks and balances all the way to the finish line to make sure things don›t go wrong. As an entrepreneur, there is no net. You see what others don't, test new ideas, seize new territory, and take risks. This requires courage, a thick skin, and the ability to keep going despite rejection and skepticism—daily!*

4. **You can't only focus on what you do best.** *When you're an employee, you can typically hone your skill set on a functional skill: accounting, law, marketing, HR, operations, admin, etc. As an entrepreneur, you wear every hat simultaneously unless you have the funds to outsource what you're not good at or don't want to do. This is one of the biggest challenges for entrepreneurs. They want to do what they do well and ignore the other areas of the business. You can be the best social media strategist, but if you don't bill and collect from your clients, you'll be out of business in short order.*

5. **You're always seeking knowledge.** *As an employee, training is often delivered to you; the company lines up continuing education, which is part of HR's job. As*

an entrepreneur, you'll have to find information on your own via online courses, books, magazines, or mentors. This can include learning to set up an accounting system, getting investors on board, marketing your ideas, crafting your perfect pitch, or using unfamiliar technology. It can be overwhelming to decide where to go to find the most relevant, actionable information, but as an entrepreneur, you must **love** *to learn—you'll be constantly immersed in gathering new information.*

6. **There is safety in numbers.** *As an employee, you may be responsible for your department's budget, but you likely don't have to obsess about the bottom line every month (unless you're in accounting). As an entrepreneur, you'd better learn to love numbers quickly because, ultimately, it's* **your** *sales, costs, and (hopefully) profits that you will determine if you survive or fail. Even more challenging can be cash flow—you might be profitable on paper, but your business can sink if you can't float month to month (especially in a product-based business).*

   IMPORTANT—I don't gravitate to numbers, so this is the first thing I hired someone else to do. For me, it's well worth the money to pay, not only a good bookkeeper to keep my records straight, but also a CFO to sit my butt down on a monthly basis and go over the numbers with me. This is money well spent!

7. **You better love it.** *As an employee, you can go on doing something you dislike just for the salary. As an entrepreneur, you must be* **passionate** *about your business because of the effort and long hours required. You*

must consistently remind yourself of your "why": **why** *are you doing this? What bigger purpose are you serving? Thomas Edison once said, "I never did a day's work in my life. It was all fun!"*

8. **Bring on the rebel.** *As an employee, your focus is on following the rules. If you don't, you'll be punished or even fired. There's little or no room for imagination. As an entrepreneur, you need to think of yourself as a rebel! You must always be looking for ways to do things differently. Perfection is the enemy of good enough. You must take shortcuts, find loopholes, and do more with less. You must be resourceful and even sometimes scrappy!*

9. **You control your time.** *Most employees are required to be at the office during a certain time frame. For some employers, you must simply show your face, even if your work is done. As an entrepreneur, you decide when you work and where you work, but don't think it will be a picnic. You will (and should) work harder than you've ever worked before. You will always be thinking about your business, what it's doing well, and what it could be doing better. You will dream it, live it, and breathe it.*

10. **Just do it.** *Most people underestimate the time it really takes to launch a business, so it makes sense to start now. If you can just get up one hour earlier each day and spend time planning and building your new business, this could give you the opportunity to develop skills and build experience while still enjoying the safety net of a salary—which, at some point, you will almost certainly need to give up if you want to grow your business.*

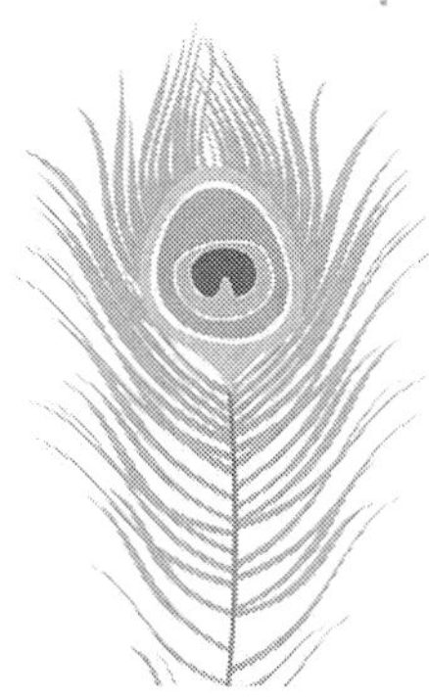

Acknowledgments

I COULDN'T HAVE DONE this without the Hera Hub team behind me, guiding and mentoring through the writing process! Rachel Kowalski, Freewave Productions, writer and content developer, as well as one of my biggest cheerleaders. Beth Riley, BARdamiss Communications, the fastest editor in the West. And Donna Kozik, book writing and marketing coach—we started together and ended together!

To Silvia Mah, founder of Hera Labs and Hera Angels, for helping me build the Hera empire.

I'm grateful for so many amazing friends both in and out of the Hera Hub community—many members who have now become my friends.

To Keith Lazerson, an amazing man and best general contractor in Southern California, who helped me with everything related to *building* my entrepreneurial dreams! And to Vanessa Wilde, my interior goddess, who helped me with the flow and feel of each of our beautiful Hera Hub locations.

And I'm most grateful for an inspiring mother and fantastic father who, despite a few bumps in the road, raised a confident, resilient REBEL!

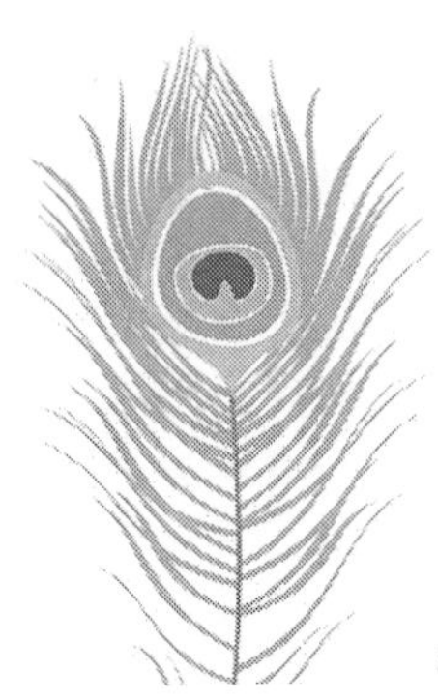

About the Author

Felena is a long-time entrepreneur and marketing maven. Her latest venture, Hera Hub, is a spa-inspired shared workspace and community for female entrepreneurs. This as-needed, flexible work and meeting space provides a productive environment for growing businesses. Hera Hub members have access to a professional space to meet with clients and to connect and collaborate with like-minded business owners, thus giving them the support they need to be prosperous. The business supports hundreds of freelancers, entrepreneurs, and nonprofits in over 16 industry segments.

Felena and Hera Hub have been featured in Inc Magazine, the BBC News, Forbes, and the New York Times. After building three successful locations, she is now expanding across the United States via a licensing model. Her goal is to support over 20,000 women in the launch and growth of their business by 2020.

Learn more at www.Felena.com and www.HeraHub.com

Made in the USA
Middletown, DE
28 January 2019